OPERATION BREWERY
BLACK HOPS - THE LEAST COVERT OPERATION IN BREWING

A step-by-step guide to building
a brewery on a budget

Dan Norris

with Eddie Oldfield and Michael McGovern

CONTENTS

JOIN US IN THE
BLACK HOPS AMBASSADOR GROUP

There's a lot covered in this book, and many of these topics are better discussed with a community of like-minded brewers and business people.

If you would like to delve into these topics further, we have a free Black Hops Ambassador group on Facebook. We help members out with questions about brewing and business and members help us when we need a hand. Win-win!

Visit blackhops.com.au/ambassadors and request to join. We'll see you there.

WHAT THIS BOOK IS, AND WHAT IT ISN'T

Hey, it's Dan here, one of the founders of Black Hops Brewery. When we set out to build a brewery, we decided to document every step along the way. I've written books before, so it wasn't long before we decided it would be a good idea to turn our lessons into a book.

Starting and running any business is complicated, and it's always difficult to decide when one of your lessons is useful to someone else. My life in business has taught me that what happens to someone else is not necessarily going to happen to me. What works for them might not work for me; what they fail at might be what I succeed at.

Still, it's invaluable to learn as much as you can before you delve into starting a business, particularly one that will cost hundreds of thousands of dollars. You will see what I mean when you see our finances!

This book was intentionally completed right when we opened. It's full of stories and lessons from us on our journey from making homebrew to opening our own brewery. It means we don't cover things relating to running a brewery like pricing, distribution, sales, hiring, etc. It also means that it's an accurate and real account of what we went through on the road leading up to opening, with no sugarcoating and no hindsight.

We hope the stories in this book are entertaining, useful, and maybe even inspiring. Remember, these are our lessons and your experience will be very different to ours.

Although this has been written in my own voice, this project was started and worked on by Michael (Govs), Eddie, and me.

Supporters

By the time you read this, we will be open and selling beer on the Gold Coast. That would not be possible without a *lot* of epic people.

Paul, Teneille, Sam, and Biebs

Our investors, Sam, Paul, and Paul's wife Teneille, backed us when we were three guys with a dream. We would not have been able to open Black Hops without them, and we are eternally grateful for their support. Our landlord, Biebs, has been our number one supporter from the beginning.

Friends and family

All of us have had epic support from our friends and family; thanks for being part of the journey with us. We decided not to mention names specifically here, but you know who you are.

Black Hops Ambassadors

We have a Facebook group called The Black Hops Ambassadors. The members are super active and have helped us promote Black Hops, particularly during our crowdfunding campaign. Thanks, Ambassadors!

Pozible backers

At the start of 2016, we ran a crowdfunding campaign to help us open the doors. Here is a full list of the epic contributors. Thanks so much for backing us to get it done and for being part of our journey.

During our Pozible campaign, we had a reward for $500 for five cartons of beer. We had two legends step up and take that reward. Nathan Chan from Foundr Magazine, a good friend of mine, and Scott Imlach from Bine Bar and Dining, a good friend to all three of us. Legends!

Here is a full list of the Pozible backers:

Luke Marshall, Zeb Ede, Chris O'Halloran, Kristi Barrow, Wendy Papas, Stirling Howland, Esther McGovern, Helen Edwards, Marcus Marais, James Graham, Paul Soady, Toby Jenkins, Jennie Gordon, Corrie Glen, Jeremy Dwyer, John Musker, John Murphy, Daniel Middler, Nick Bonner, Loretta McGill, Will Mullins, Goldtoast Supper-Club, Keith Farrell, Xavier Verhoeven, Phil Guilletmot, Nat Burcher, Adam Passfield, Nathan Bowes, Matthew Coomber, Adam Sewell, Jenna, Paul and Teneille Simpson, Michael Carlsen, Stephen Cooper, Peter Wheldon, Hayden Brass, Mick Byrne, Emma Papas, Ben France, John McGovern, Adrian Strutton, Claire Oldfield, Gordon McGregor, Dylan Robinson,

Dave Curtis, Luke Ronalds, Sean Reynolds Massey-Reed, Tommy and Mary Miller, Christopher Hey, Mark Moffatt, Joy Townsend, John Elliott, Tegan Knight, Scott McLean, Matthew McGavern, Gary Andrew and Joanne Kennett, Laetitia Somers, Matt Dick, Rohan Dutton, Craig Maiden, Nick Barnes, Scott Garnett, Luke Shield, Beards Meat Beer, Chris Chamberlain, Chris Wormald, Matthew Beggs, Simon Pilkington, Nicholas Pandelakis, Michael Walker, James Traill, Brad Hardy, Jarrod Robinson, Adam Coburn, Matthew Jackson, Nicole Box, Anne and Steve Carlin, Gareth Latham, Murray Francis, Martin and Pauline Oldfield, Aaron Birkby, Darren Hastie, Melina Wornes, Dean Boughen, Jo Espey, Philip Nelson, Mike Shaw, Kathleen Ho, Gary Fletcher, Troy Thompson, Matt and Ingrid Flanagan, Jamie Pollard, Joshua Loftus, Scott Shomer, Alan Hayes, Matthew Thomas, Gordon Smith, David Lawrence, Sarah Swinton, Andy Chilton, Ronson Blake, Rory Delaney, Ben McAdam, Damian Rigby, Matt Farrelly, Chad, Chris Marks, Michael Carlsen, Dave Perry, John Dunlea, Chris O'Halloran, Gareth Russell, Paul Soady, Nick Bonner, David Lardner, Jamie Brocket, David Kitchen, Sjon (Kegs) Wakeham, Adrian Carrales, Ryan Daniel, Dinan Gunawardena, Leith Booker, Jared Oldfield, Steven Sonsino, Tom Morkes, Miranda Packer, Kieran Ord, Robert McGinn, Chris Marr, Mark Reid, Mark William Davies, David Black, Samantha Morris, David Scott Kane, Sean Johnson, Vic Dorfman, Nick Davis, Rob Walling, James Welham, Michael Kirchhubel, Jeremy Chandanais, Adedayo Charis, Chris Varnom, Xavier Verhoeven, Paul Kemp, Trent Martin, Tim Yarham, Scott Kilmartin, Matty Oakes, Georgie Seddon, Meg Solly, Bradley McCarty, Alex Kelly, David Hindin, Debz and Moog, Jess Mcwatt Forbes, Mark Willetts, Erica and Kieran Ryan, Claire Dryden, Judd Owen, Rob McDonald, Jason Poffley, Murray, Anna Webb, Kim Doyal, Cameron James, Corey Lardner, Zac Smith, and Melissa Murray.

HQ helpers

When building the brewery, we had a lot of people come and give us a hand. Here is a list of the main suspects, but thank you to everyone who popped in.

Matt Vergotis, Matthew Dick, Chris Chamberlain, Fiona Ramiah, Dave Orbell, Claire Oldfield, Martin and Pauline Oldfield, Kieran Ryan, Linden Prescott, Jeremy James, Jesse Curry, Pete Wheldon, Tom Russell, Luke Ronalds, Mark Beck, Jon Kruger, Byron Hall, Mushy, Eamonn McGovern, Dave Dwyer, Russell Steele, Clive Oldfield, Claire Dryden, and Mark (Trouty) Traucnnieks.

Press

We've also had a lot of press, particularly from local Gold Coast outlets and beer and food blogs. Thanks to More Gold Coast, Inside Gold Coast, Gold Coast Bulletin, Courier Mail, Metropolist Gold Coast, The Crafty Pint, Weekend Edition Gold Coast, Craft Beer Reviewer, Brews News, Brewed Crude and Bitter, 250 Beers, From Gold Blog, FROTH mag, and Blank Gold Coast.

Bars

We wouldn't exist if we didn't have bars selling our beer. Thanks to all of the bars that have sold Black Hops. In particular, we'd like to thank: Ze Pickle, who were the first to offer our beer on the Gold Coast; HooHa Bar, who were the first in Brisbane; Bine Bar and Dining and Lester & Earl on the Gold Coast, who have supported us at every step.

FOREWORD
BY STEVE 'HENDO' HENDERSON

Building a brewery and making awesome beer. Sounds like the world's best job, right? I mean, surely, it can't be much more than just sitting around the brewery all day drinking beer, yeah?

Reality check, folks—there's a lot more to it than that. While homebrewing is a bucket load of fun, imagine being a homebrewer who suddenly decides that he or she is going to go into the craft beer business. What a brilliant idea! That's so awesome! But, all of a sudden, your hobby is your profession. It's something that keeps you awake at night as you try to work out if your beer is being made to your exacting standard of quality, whether or not you're selling enough, and how you're going to pay your next lot of excise duty to the ATO (Australian Taxation Office).

If introducing the complexity and stress of money into your hobby floats your boat, then this book is for you. If you're happy creating awesome homebrews for your mates on the weekend, then there's nothing wrong with that either. Enjoy the read. Enjoy the home-brewing. Save me a beer.

So, why get into the craft beer industry in the first place? When I first met Dan, Eddie, and Govs a couple of years ago in Brisbane, we spoke about how they were going to "start something" on the Gold Coast. I've spoken to countless people who, after a few too many beers, say the same thing. For most, it's just a pipe dream and something that never comes to fruition. For some, the challenge of making some great beer and showing them to the world is just too much to resist.

I recall when I decided to start my own brewing company back in 2012 with great excitement and trepidation. Armed with only a few years of brewing experience, a few good beer recipes, and nowhere near enough cash, I created BrewCult. I couldn't afford to build a brewery of my own, so I became a "gypsy brewer," which means that I used other breweries' equipment to make my beer. This is the business model BrewCult continues to run by today.

With a determination to build a brewing company that made innovative and exciting beers, I dove head first into the craft beer industry. I figured, *If I make the beer, then surely people will just buy it.* While there are a small subset of customers out there who will buy your beer just because you are new or local, this will only get you so far.

Countless sleepless nights later, BrewCult enjoys national distribution and recently won the inaugural "Champion Gypsy Brewer" Trophy at the 2016 Australian International Beer Awards (AIBAs).

Getting there was no easy task.

Over the last four years, I have learnt a lot about the liquor industry, including branding, sales, marketing, procurement, financial management, and logistics. None of these things have anything to do with the brewing of beer. For me, brewing is the easy part.

For you, making good beer is super important. Our consumers pay a premium price for craft beer and they deserve a well-made product. Make a shitty beer and give it to someone that's new to craft beer and they'll instinctively know it. It's almost like us human beings are naturally gifted with spidey sense to detect crappy beer. Give someone who's new to craft beer a shitty beer and that person will go back to their generic lager and never ever come back. That reflects poorly, not only on yourself, but for the rest of us in the industry.

Please, don't do that to your beer. Don't do that to your peers in the industry, and please, don't do that to me. Good beer needs more than just a creative recipe. Make your beer with a quality focus. If you can, get a formal education to learn how to make beer well.

I look fondly at my friends Dan, Eddie, and Govs and the journey that they have embarked on. Though Black Hops started out as a gypsy-brewer outfit like BrewCult, it was their dream to ultimately build and operate their own brewery. Being temporary gypsy brewers merely gave the brand a quick go-to-market. Smart move.

People all over the world are flocking to craft beer. The craft beer industry in Australia makes up less than 5% of the total beer market, yet this small subset of the industry is currently enjoying double-digit growth. Why is this happening? Consumers are demanding more choice and diversity in what beer they choose to drink, and they also want to know who makes their beer and where it is made.

This demand is driving a whole new diversity in beer styles and ways of brewing beer. Everybody wins. Yay for diversity! Yay for choice!

Among all that diversity, this book describes the Black Hops journey. Their story is one way to set up a craft beer business. You might look to follow in their footsteps, or you might choose a different path.

Will you open a brewery and get rich quick? Absolutely not. While our customers are paying a premium for beer, the margins are slim for brewers and the costs are forward thanks to our system of taxation.

Case in point: When the Black Hops boys talk about how a 2,000-litre beer tank costs about $10,000, that's pretty accurate. Now consider that they have to fill it with beer. That costs about $15,000. You empty and fill your tanks about every two weeks, and it can take up to 90 days to get all your money back from the beer that you make and sell. Think about that: Every. Two. Weeks. 90. Days. Do the sums there. $15,000 x 20 = $300,000 per tank per year. You might spend a pretty penny on a shiny new brew house, but do you have 300 large to spend on making beer?

Dan, Govs, and Eddie have built Black Hops Brewery, and now it's all up and running. Theirs is a great story and one that I truly admire. Have their challenges ended now that they're up and running? Not by a long shot! But just to make it to this point in their history shows that they are determined and driven to succeed. You, too, will need to be as hungry as the Black Hops boys if your plans are to be more than just a beer-driven pipe dream.

CHAPTER 1

EGGNOG WHAT?

1300 Hours - 26 August 2014: Fortitude Brewing, Mount Tamborine

Fuck, here we go again. That's me, in my head, after hearing yet another big idea.

I spent four years in employment. As an employee, I liked to talk about ideas a lot. In fact, my best mate, Eddie, and I spent countless hours dreaming up ideas when we worked for the government. It had been eight years since I left, and over time, my patience for "new ideas" had grown thin.

In the entrepreneurial world, I heard a new idea every day, often from the same people. I learned long ago that the people who got ahead didn't talk a lot about their ideas—they just went out and got shit done.

Still. There's a time and a place, and sitting at Fortitude Brewing at Mount Tamborine, is as good a place as any to brainstorm ideas—especially beer ideas.

"Do you reckon a stout with eggnog characteristics would work?" Eddie asked the boys. "Not sweet and sickly but a dry stout with subtle characteristics of what you find in eggnog: brandy, cinnamon, nutmeg, and vanilla."

I did what I always do when I heard a good idea: acknowledge that it's an acceptable idea and say do it, knowing full well that the person with the idea has no idea how to do it and would give up before making it a reality anyway. But this time it was different.

Eddie and I had chatted about this beer before. He had actually suggested it to other breweries but couldn't get anyone to brew it. But this time, Govs—who was a brewer at Fortitude and a mate of ours—was in company. On top of that, he'd just scraped together all of the pieces necessary to brew a decent beer at home. This included a full three-vessel Heat Exchange Recirculating Mash System (HERMS) system made from converted 50-litre beer kegs and a series of pumps and hoses he had frankensteined together. It resembled something out of Breaking Bad. He hadn't brewed on the equipment yet and was looking for an opportunity to put the rig to the test. It was a perfect storm of sorts.

Still, we certainly weren't the first blokes to sit in the pub talking about making beer and we wouldn't be the last. I didn't think about that conversation too much after that.

As I write this, a year or so on from that conversation, I am sitting in a South China Airlines flight enjoying a warm "Excellent Quality" Yanjing Beer (that's all I know about it, the rest is in Chinese). It's Eddie, Govs, and me and we are flying from Brisbane to Guangzhou to inspect our recently purchased 2,000-litre brewery.

If you are reading this book, it means that approximately 18 months after that initial conversation, we now own a brewery and there are probably other people around Australia right now talking shit and drinking our beer, Black Hops. We have investors, we have our own equipment and location, a cellar door, customers all around the country, and we've brewed the official beer for one of the biggest video games on the planet.

It's been a crazy ride. At times, Google has been our friend. At other times, we've relied on mates and colleagues to help us figure out the puzzle of building a craft beer brewery and brand. From day one, our passion has always been to share everything we are doing along the way. The tagline "The Least Covert Operation in Brewing" is something we've lived by. We've made it our mission to make it easier for others who want to do what we've done and get more people brewing, selling, and drinking high-quality beer.

Making it real

I hadn't given a second thought to Eddie's big idea, but two weeks after that boozy Mount Tamborine conversation, he sent me this message: "We're heading up the mountain to brew the Eggnog Stout, wanna come?"

I couldn't quite believe that this drunken conversation had actually led to us planning to brew beer. I immediately said yes and we headed up to Govs' place to see what we could do. His partner at the time, Claire, had kindly made her yoga room available to us as the pilot brewery location. Whether she knew about the arrangement, I'm not sure, but the space was now full of brewing equipment.

For the most part, Eddie and I watched and listened as Govs pieced his pilot system together, brewed the beer, and gave us a first-class brewing education at the same time. Aside from a few unexpected leaks, everything went to plan, and we organised to get back together for bottling in three weeks.

Three weeks is a long time in these days of modern communication. Assuming you are awake 15 hours a day and you send 12 messages per hour, you can technically communicate over 2,500 times per day. And that's pretty much what we did.

At first, the messages were practical. We'd ask about dry hopping, how to make the spiced brandy mix, how the beer was fermenting, etc. But before long, we got a little bit carried away. "What are we going to call our brewery?" "Do we need a website?" "Do we need investors?" and occasionally, after a few beers at the surf club, "Fuck this! This beer is going to be better than every single beer on sale here. Be fucked if I'm drinking this shit anymore. How do we get this into bars?!!!"

They were all good questions but the one that got the most attention was, "What are we going to call it?" If we knew that, surely it wouldn't be that hard to print labels and put a few photos on social media?

We sent hundreds of messages back and forth on this topic. Some of the names were good. Some of them were fucking atrocious (Three Balls Brewing, Mad Robot). But in the midst of mostly shocking business names, Eddie messaged, "What about Black Hops?"

We loved this name, for the obvious play on words, and so from then on we were known as Black Hops Brewing. It didn't take long before I'd mocked up a logo, registered a domain, and had the Eggnog Stout labels ready to print.

When bottling day came around, we were able to bottle the beers as well as throw on labels. They looked pretty damn sexy, I must say. We distributed the bottles among ourselves, and agreed to meet at Eddie's place in two weeks for the initial tasting.

After brewing homebrew in my youth and also drinking some of Australia's best beers in the months leading up to the brew, I wasn't sure what to expect. In the midst of the 2,500+ messages, there must have been 100 of this one from me: "What do you think it's going to taste like?"

I had 100% faith in Govs, but at the same time, he was brewing his first homebrew on the most ghetto equipment imaginable. I kind of thought it would taste like the homebrew from my youth, but I was also hoping we'd see some potential.

We had a new level of expectation considering this was now the first beer for Black Hops Brewing and the pic was going straight to Instagram after tasting it!

I'm not exactly sure when we went from talking complete shit to actually being serious about brewing beer, but I think it was about then.

When Eddie popped the top off the first beer and we smelled the waft of cinnamon, nutmeg, and vanilla, it was game on.

Game on

We didn't have huge expectations for that first brew. It all sounded amazing, but I don't know if any of us really expected the beer to taste exactly how Eddie described it on Mount Tamborine that day.

But it did. The eggnog characteristics of nutmeg, cinnamon, brandy, and vanilla were there on the nose, and it drank like a solid, sessionable dry stout. Govs is never 100% happy with a beer, there's always something that can be better, so he had something to experiment with. But for Eddie and I, it tasted literally exactly how we hoped and how he described it.

We created a Black Hops account on the craft beer app, Untappd, and we were ready to share it with the world.

We put it on our own social media accounts and we started talking about it to our friends. We sent a few bottles off to people in the local craft beer scene as samples. We hoped they would drink the beer and, ideally, like it! What happened was a lot more exciting. They drank it, they loved it, they shared pics, and they wrote about it!

One of our friends, Darren, is a local blogger called 250 Beers. Eddie met him at the Pig 'N' Whistle in Brisbane for a sneaky lunchtime Pac Ale and gave him a bottle of the Eggnog Stout. We delivered it in a brown paper bag and were legitimately interested in his discerning opinion. A few weeks later, we were walking down George Street, Sydney, on a boys-only craft beer ~~bender~~ research trip, when Eddie got a notification on Facebook that 250 Beers had posted an article on us. We were beyond stoked! This was our first article, and not only was it good publicity for us, it also made us believe we could do this.

Darren is a top bloke, incredibly supportive, and an important part of the Queensland/Australian craft beer scene. We were sweating on his opinion. These were his words:

"To say that I was pleasantly surprised is an understatement. You see, I popped the cap with a sense of trepidation. I really wanted it to be good.

I really wanted to be happy for Eddie but I feared that I'd be greeted by nothing more than a decent homebrew. I needn't have worried. It was very good. Delicious and tasty - it was more than I'd hoped for... The guys have set the bar very high with Eggnog Stout so I imagine there's a rather loud buzz of expectation circling the Gold Coast right about now."

Darren also posted a pic on Instagram, and checked it in on the Untappd app along with a rating of four stars. This attention led to other people doing the same thing and things grew from there. Before long, we had a website, registered social media accounts, and were regularly being asked when we would sell the Eggnog Stout commercially.

That's when the real work began. It's one thing to make a batch of drinkable homebrew. It's another to figure out how to make it commercially—let alone building a brewery! This book is the culmination of everything we've learned in the 18 months since then. It's our best effort to make it an easier job for others to do the same thing that we've done.

Let's begin.

CHAPTER 2

HOW TO BUILD A BRAND

Whether we knew it at the time or not, from that first meeting at Mount Tamborine we were actively building our brand. Yes, we threw a quick logo together and slapped it on a bottle, but there's a lot more to it than that.

In this chapter, I'll outline everything we did to enable you to do the same thing. I've presented them in order of most important first.

Story

Any time you buy anything, you are buying into a story. Whether it's beer, a new car, a new phone, or a house—it doesn't matter. You've been told a story, or you've told one to yourself about what you are buying. And there's a good chance you've told a lot of other people as well. Stories are how businesses grow.

To build a brand you need to tell your story and present it in a way that will encourage others to share it. In our case, our story is about three guys who decided to start a brewery. We shared everything we learned along the way with a passion for helping others do the same. We did it by putting up blog posts and podcasts about what we were doing; we attended local events, generated press, and told our story through our beer descriptions and labels. Turns out the media love a good story, so every chance we got we told our story to anyone who wanted to cover us.

If you want to build a brand, stories are where it starts.

Choosing a name

We went through hundreds of names before arriving at Black Hops. The obvious play on words Black Ops (a military abbreviation of Black Operations) was nice—it was also short and easy to say—but most importantly, it worked well with our story. We wanted to build this brewery with transparency and share everything we were doing because we felt there was too much secrecy in the industry. Every time we wanted to do anything, we couldn't find any good information on how to do it, so we decided to create it and, at the same time, share it all publicly.

"Black Hops: The Least Covert Operation in Brewing" became a catchy title for us and a way we could easily explain what we were doing.

It's unlikely that a name will make or break a business, but having a great name is very useful. I'd tell people about our business and often be greeted with, "Ha, cool name." It became memorable and an easy way for them to tell other people.

Here are a few things to think about in coming up with a name:

1. Short and simple is better.
2. Make sure it sounds like the sort of thing you'd buy in a shop and talk about.

3. Think about how you might present it on a label and how that might look. Some names are hard to design for.

4. Check that the name and the domain is either available or acquirable. Lots of domains are taken, but if no one is actively using it, you may be able to acquire it. This may mean local or international trademark searches or local business register searches depending on how far you are planning on taking it.

5. Make sure you like it because you'll be saying it a lot! And until you build up a recognised brand, you'll be judged on it.

Logo

Our design process was very long and extremely painful, but we were more than stoked with the end result. Early on, I designed the logo myself and it worked for us for the first year or so before we launched seriously.

We went through six designers before we found one that could make something that we thought was better than the one I did. We didn't want to compromise on our design. In the end, we had to pay a pretty hefty sum for a very high-quality local designer, Matt Vergotis, to help us get our branding right.

For a commercial packaged product, I think this is money well spent. We provided Matt with a document that talked about what we were looking for and what we liked and didn't like in other beer designs. We did a bottle shop tour and a lot of back and forth emails and messages. We wanted something modern and elegant but also something that would stand out.

We asked him for a simple logo and one that would work well on labels for beers ranging from big black beers with military names like ABC Bomb to sessionable summer beers like our Beach House Ale. It was a big challenge, but Matt was up to it.

We specified early on that we wanted to have final access to the source files to make small changes, which is critical if you don't want to be stuck with the same designer your whole life. In my experience, most design processes don't go according to plan, so this is something you should insist on.

Our design process included:

- A logo "Black Hops"
- A monogram that we could use when we couldn't use the full logo
- 6 labels/decal designs for our core range
- Editable source files to enable us to produce all of the various versions we needed. This would include various sizes and shapes for social media profiles, presentations, the website, and lots of other things we hadn't even thought of when we started the process.

Here are a few tips during the design process:

- Learn about design yourself, and look at how the best companies in the world put their brands forward. Don't pretend to be an expert, but respect the craft and make sure you can tell the difference between something that is well done and something that isn't. Start paying attention to everything you see, and start thinking about why it works/doesn't work.
- Everyone will want to be your designer and everyone thinks they are a design expert. The best thing you can do is find a legitimately world-class designer, and they

probably won't be cheap. Look at their past work, and make sure they are suitable for a business like yours.

- Meet them and make sure you think you could go through a difficult process with them.
- Don't post three logos on Facebook and ask your mates which one they like best. Include key people like the founders and investors in the decision-making process. Your mates don't know design, and they will lead you astray.
- Think about your design in context. Don't look at a logo in isolation. Look at the full label actually printed at a bar or on a bottle. Something might look good on the screen, but it might be a different story in person. A good designer should include this in the process.
- Think about the kind of story you want to tell with your design and the way you want people to feel when they see your product. This is the essence of design; it's not just making something pretty.
- If you don't love it, don't agree to it. It's 100% essential that all of the founders love your branding. It took us a long time to get to that stage, but it was worth it.
- Don't expect the process to be easy, but expect to get a high-quality result at the end.

Forging a relationship with Matt ended up being a major plus for us. He helped us with several more design projects before opening, including special release beer decals and even hand-drawing our new logo at the cellar door.

Having great design is a must for any startup, so finding a good designer early is very important.

Decals/labels

We got started by designing and printing our own tap decals and bottle labels on a small scale at a local printer. We started putting these labels on our early homebrews just to add a bit of credibility to what we were doing.

Once we had the logo professionally re-designed, we also had decals and labels printed properly. We wanted to respect the design process and get something that would really grab attention at bars and in bottle shops.

There are lots of options when it comes to decals, handles, and packaged products. The options below are the simplest and cheapest ways to get started, but do your research and figure out what works for you. Keep in mind that expensive decals and labels will increase lead time and cost in the product. Decals often get lost and need to be re-printed. Bars expect to have enough of them handy for when they put your beer on.

If you want to go the DIY option, we have a few templates that might help. You can grab them as downloadable files at blackhops.com.au/book. Ultimately, you will want to talk to the professionals and get high-quality decals and labels printed.

In the beginning, we only did low-volume printing, and therefore, the commercial printing options were out. We chatted to a few places who provided exorbitant quotes, then found a local print shop to do the small-volume labels.

It was near our place and could do very small print jobs, which meant we could get them at late notice and for our full range of products. Longer term, we moved to a supplier who could handle larger volumes.

For really small runs, we used a local company called Varsity Graphics. For bigger runs, we used another local provider called Graffiti Stickers, and for the final print labels, we used an even larger scale provider called Graphix.

First, it was laminated card circles, then we moved to EVA foam rectangle decals, and once we opened, we started looking at the clear dome decals.

Stickers

People love stickers, so we had a bunch made up to give away. A lot of people will put them on cars so make sure they are high quality. We included stickers in our crowdfunding campaign, so we had them printed for that. It's hard to make money from stuff like this, but if you have super fans that want to put stickers on their cars, it's a good idea to have them available.

Bar runners and coasters

We had bar runners and coasters printed for our cellar door by a local company, Just Coolers. The coasters were super cheap and the bar runners weren't too expensive either. Coasters are a useful marketing tool, so we had a bunch printed, and we handed them out to bars who wanted to use them.

Banners, posters, and business cards

We used VistaPrint to print a whole bunch of things from business cards to big banners for events. When we needed fast and high-quality printing we used local providers. But if it could wait a week and the quality wasn't a huge factor, VistaPrint were the cheapest and best option.

Caps, shirts, and more

We also had shirts and caps done. People love it when you give them a free shirt and we have had quite a few people buy the shirts, even before we opened. We used an online service called The Print Bar who could print and ship the shirts on demand. We also ordered a bunch from a local printer that we could either sell or take with us and give away to people. This was cheaper per shirt, but we had to send them out ourselves, which takes extra time and money.

When we opened the physical location, we kept them on hand for people to buy. We had big plans to sell the shirts at events and online, but in reality, we ended up wearing them ourselves and giving most of them away.

It's good advertising, but it does add up when you are getting runs of 20 or 30 shirts done and giving most of them away.

Website

Luckily, I have a web design/development background, so putting a website up on WordPress was one of the first things we did. In fact, we had a website before we even had our first homebrew!

Building it in WordPress and hosting it ourselves meant it could grow with us. Early on, it was just a homepage and a contact page. By the time we opened, it had a number of pages, including our beer list, an online store, and a home for our blog and podcast—all built around the same platform we started with.

We were getting around 4,000 visits per month at opening time and ranking on the front page of Google for most of the major beer keywords in our area.

There is a lot of bad advice around when it comes to websites and online marketing. I've run businesses in this space for the last 10 years, and this is really all I ever do when I set up a new website:

1. Use WordPress so it can grow infinitely as the business grows.
2. Make sure I use a nice-looking theme that looks great on all of the popular devices.
3. Make sure it's optimised for speed. This is important for customers and for rankings in Google and is becoming increasingly vital as phone usage and impatience increases!
4. Make sure it's optimized for conversions, meaning it does a good job at prompting people to take action of some kind, such as opting into the email list.
5. Make sure it's loaded up with quality content that is better than the competition.

The key part of all of this is really the content. There's less and less point in having a website these days without decent content. People can find your contact details on Facebook, message you on Facebook, Twitter, Instagram, and Snapchat and find your story in Google. A site makes you look more legitimate for sure, but the main benefit of having a site in 2016 is the ability to build authority and an audience by publishing your own content.

This is called content marketing and it's a personal passion of mine, so I delve into it more in Chapter Seven - Marketing.

CHAPTER 3

WHAT DO YOU NEED TO START A BREWERY?

Now all this talk of branding has gotten us far away from why we are here in the first place: making beer. Let's delve into what you need to start a brewing business.

Since opening, we've talked at a lot of events about how to start a brewery, and we've met with a lot of people who are involved in the process. We've also followed the journeys of successful and unsuccessful brewing startups in Australia and overseas. Brewing is not an easy business; there are a lot of forces working against you.

My background is in online business, and I can tell you it's much easier making money from online products and services than beer. But of course it's nowhere near as much fun!

Here are the things that we think you absolutely need to have if you want to start a brewing business and have any chance at success.

A point of difference

With everything I've done in business over the last 10 years, from embarrassing failures to "overnight" successes, one thing has been consistent: it's not good enough to be better, you have to be different.

Every successful startup in the world is somehow different to their competitors in ways that their customers care about. Apple have relied on design and product innovation, Tesla produce Ferrari-beating SUVs that use no petrol, Uber costs 40% less than a taxi and come to you with a simple tap on your phone.

These points of difference are what get people talking about you and your business.

With the beer business, it's a smaller scale, but it's no different. You need some way of getting attention. For us, it was our story, three guys making craft beer and sharing everything we learn. News outlets loved the story and our branding and name, Black Hops. Every opportunity we got, we looked for new ways of telling our story.

We also innovated on beer styles and produced beers that people weren't familiar with, such as an Australian take on a French Saison, as well as our initial Eggnog Stout.

The other breweries that we looked up to, differentiated in some way as well:

- Brew Dog had a TV show and used their attitude and humor to build a worldwide audience.
- More locally, Stone & Wood paved the way for craft beer with their unique Pacific Ale.

- Balter Brewers opened nearby and were headed up by Mick Fanning and a bunch of the world's best surfers.

These points of difference become unique stories and the press and your customers latch onto them and spread them like wildfire.

If there's nothing different about what you are doing, you are not likely to succeed in the brewing business.

Commercial brewing experience

You would think it would go without saying that having experience brewing in a commercial brewery would be a prerequisite for starting a brewing business. But it's amazing how many people have approached us about starting their own brewery who don't have this.

You absolutely need to know how to make good beer in a commercial setting if you want to make it in the brewing business. You could give up some equity for a good brewer, or hire one, but the best case is that you have a brewer on your founding team.

For us, we were lucky that Govs had that well and truly covered. The normal path we see is people homebrewing for years before gradually working their way into the commercial brewing industry. With Govs, that first pilot batch of Eggnog Stout was actually the first homebrew he had ever made. He'd been working for Queensland's largest craft breweries for seven years and that was his bread and butter.

Govs' knowledge is mind blowing. It's not just making the weird and wonderful creations we made early on with the homebrew setup, it's also scaling it to a full commercial size batch. That process is always going to be difficult, and a lot riskier without a solid knowledge and experience in making commercial beer.

Doing some homebrew batches for your mates won't cut it, and your mates telling you that your beer is great won't cut it either. I learned long ago not to listen to what people tell you in business. Instead, you need to watch what they do. Your mates telling you that your beer is great is not validation. People purchasing it in a commercial setting is.

A great founding team

It's virtually impossible to start a great business by yourself. In the startup world, incubators and investors will laugh you out of the room if you are there by yourself. Great businesses need a great team, and this is especially the case in brewing because of the vast array of work that has to be done. Making great beer is just the beginning.

Here are a few skills you will need to have covered within your founding team:

1. Product design - This involves everything that goes into thinking up, designing, executing, and selling a beer. Branding, presentation, and how the market perceives the beer will all need to be considered. With Black Hops, Eddie and Govs have both contributed equally in coming up with a bunch of innovative beer recipes. Govs has managed to nail it every time on our little pilot setup and as we scaled up to a full-sized system.
2. Relationships - Eddie and Govs are both well-known people in the craft beer community, and I'm well known in online circles. They have done a great job at building the

right relationships with people to a point where people pay attention to what we do and are keen to help. I've continued that work online to a point where we were well known long before we opened our physical location. Community and relationship building is a critical skill, and I'll delve into that more in its own chapter.

3. Design and printing - Having an understanding of design and printing is essential in a physical business. Early on, it was up to us to design our logo, get it onto the right format for packaging, and hack together decals and keg collars. Once we were serious, we had a designer professionally design all of it, but I still have to regularly jump into Photoshop or Illustrator and get my hands dirty. We are forever printing decals and keg collars and organizing other merch like stickers and shirts. Having these skills in-house is very handy; it means we can get the experts to do the hardcore creative design work, and we can do the more manual Photoshop work. Having the technical skills probably isn't essential, but having an eye for design is. It's too easy to be led astray by bad designers and friends and family when it comes to design.

4. Online - The online world can't be ignored anymore. I run a web support company and have been building sites for 10 years. This has ensured that everything we have done with our website has been without hassle and virtually free, and we've been able to execute an online marketing strategy that is best in class.

5. Content and social media - The world has changed with phones and mobile apps, and social media is how people spend their attention these days. Being able to build an audience on social media is essential, and staying on top of what's happening on a weekly basis has become a core skill. We are on every major platform and had thousands

of followers before we opened. Having someone, or ideally all of your founding team, as pros on social media is a huge bonus. Half of the battle with social media is having the right mindset in the founding team. Too many people think it's a hassle and treat it as an afterthought. Those people are going to struggle as mass attention moves from traditional advertising outlets to mobile apps.

6. Legal/compliance - We've also had to get our head around some legal and compliance issues. Govs dealt with the ATO, Eddie organised the banking, and I've helped put together a partnership agreement and an accounting system. Having someone on your team who has run a business before is very important.

7. Marketing channel - Someone on your team has to be a gun at marketing. When I think about businesses, I consider two things: first the idea itself, and second, how the idea will be marketed. Both have equal importance. You won't be able to sell a great idea if no one knows about it, and even if everyone knows about it, you won't be able to sell a bad idea. Both need equal consideration, so if your founding team is stacked with brewers and no one knows marketing, then this is a big problem. In our case, Govs knows beer, Eddie knows people, and I know online marketing.

8. Distribution - Making a lot of noise is one thing, but at scale you will have to sell a lot of beer. Someone will have to understand, or come to understand, how that takes place. There is a lot to learn when it comes to distributing your beer around a city or country. Understanding which bars will buy from you, how to store kegs, how to efficiently transfer them interstate or deliver them locally, when to use your own kegs or rent kegs, are all part of the equation. Someone on your team will have to know this stuff and

take responsibility for making sure you can manage a lot of variables.

There's an argument to suggest that you can outsource some or all of these things. With the right amount of funding, this is probably true, but when you outsource, you will usually only get something as good as the founding team insists. If you know nothing about social media, you won't know if you are getting good social media support. I've seen companies that spend hundreds of thousands of dollars on social media and have been around for 5+ years who get significantly less traction than we do. That's why I consider these core skills as essential in-house components of your founding team.

Some equipment

Of course, if you want to brew beer you need some brewing equipment.

I think it was a good decision for us to have brewed a few pilot batches before taking things further. Govs has a pretty decent homebrew setup that was good enough for us to make some great beer.

Once we started establishing our full brewery, we had our friends Debz and Moog generously make us up a 100-litre pilot system. This enabled us to brew a full 50-litre keg pretty efficiently, which we still use at Black Hops headquarters for pilot batches.

For brewing your main commercial batches, you either need your own equipment or you need to rent someone else's. I'll delve into both these options in this book, since we did both.

Licences and regulatory requirements

You will need to be able to legally produce and sell beer in your local area. Depending on where you are, the requirements will be different. For us, we needed a producer wholesaler licence, which we set up for Eddie's house. This enabled us to brew at other breweries and sell our beer to bars.

On top of that, we needed to be running a business, which in Australia requires an Australian Business Number (ABN). We also registered for GST, which is compulsory once you are turning over $75,000 to Australian customers. Even if you are only new, it's still recommended.

Consult your local authorities to figure out exactly what you need for your location.

Somewhere to brew

There are essentially three options for brewing your first beer:

1. Do a collab brew - In this instance, it's generally released under the name of the place you brew at, although it's effectively their beer then. It's a good starting point with not much barrier to entry. All you need to do is convince a brewery to do one with you. The downside is that it's not really your beer, and if you ultimately want to build your own brand, you probably want to release your own beer. We did plenty of collab brews as we worked up to our opening, and we continue to do them. They are an awesome way to have some fun, create some social media

content, and make some great relationships. Not to mention, they often result in some awesome beer!

2. Contract brew/Gypsy brew - This is what we decided to do for our first commercial release. It involves finding a brewery and paying them to use their equipment and releasing a beer under your own name. I'll delve into this more in the next chapter. For us, it meant waiting around for a while for our licence and fronting up a bit of cash for the commercial batch. Depending on the brewery, you could possibly avoid this with a collab.

3. Get your own system - This would be a lot of fun, and you'd have complete control. But you are looking at hundreds of thousands of dollars to get started on a system that would be commercially viable. Ultimately, this is where we got to, but not without doing a lot of collab and contract batches first.

For us, the contract brew stood out as the best balance between having a crack ourselves, and not taking too much risk.

A bit of cash

At this stage, it's too hard to say how much it's going to cost to make your first beer, but you can't get it done for $0. We put about $5,000 of our own money into an account, which gave us enough to make a start on our first contract-brewed batch and everything that came along with doing that. That's cool, particularly for our first brew. We would have almost paid that much just to go into a bar and drink our own beer!

There are a number of ways to raise money for a brewery. I'll talk through the specific costs and funding options later in the book.

Logistical considerations

There are also some considerations to do with moving the beer around:

- Where the beer gets stored - In Queensland, it needs to be stored at a licenced premises. When we were contract brewing, we were leaving the kegs at the brewery and delivering them from there (which meant no additional warehousing). As we started making more beer, we moved to an off-site licenced cold storage warehouse in Brisbane called Outrayjus.
- What kegs you use and who delivers and retrieves them - In our case, we used the brewery's kegs at first before buying our own kegs and using a keg rental service called Kegstar for interstate deliveries.
- How you will deliver the kegs - Again on a small scale, locally, you can probably get away with something simple for your first batch. In the early days, we used Eddie's van and my Nissan X-Trail to deliver kegs. Depending on who you use for kegs, you may get charged for the length of time they are in use. If that's the case, you need to stay on top of when the beer is finished so you can return them.

A detailed recipe

Before we decided to make any beer, Eddie and Govs had brainstormed a recipe for the Eggnog Stout. Before we'd brewed a commercial batch of it, we'd brewed a pilot batch and had a few changes to make. Govs had also worked on much larger systems in the past.

For small pilot batches, you can be experimental, but the more beer you make, the less risk you want to take. We wanted to be very certain our first commercial batch would taste good. Our reputation was on the line with people who would hopefully become our major customers.

Community support

The craft beer community has been amazing to us so far and this industry relies heavily on relationships. You can't sell beer without great relationships with bars. You can't make beer without great relationships with hop and malt suppliers. If you want to start a business in this space, cultivating industry and community support is a must.

I'll dig into this later in the book, but for now, you should be thinking about how you can start building relationships with the general community, bars and restaurants, and suppliers.

Packaging

Once the beer is made, your job isn't done. You also have to arrange things like:

- Decals for the taps
- Keg collars for the kegs
- Bottle samples if possible

For us, we did all of this on the cheap for the first batch. We bottled the beer with a counter-pressure filler and mocked up labels to give us photos for social media. This was a very good idea; packaged photos make you look a lot more legit and the photos turned up on blogs and other places once we put them out. As we grew, we got more and more serious about our packaging.

That's not an exhaustive list, but it gives you an idea of the types of things to think about before putting beer out to market. Making the beer is only a small part of the equation. In the next chapter, we'll dig into the detailed steps we took to get our first beer to market.

CHAPTER 4

OUR FIRST COMMERCIAL BREW

I've run through a summary of what I think you need to start a brewing company, but let's get into the details of how we did it.

Pilot batches

We left the Black Hops story just after we released our first home-brew of Eggnog Stout. As we progressed more on the branding, and more stories were written about the beer, our priority turned to putting out a commercial release. The homebrew became known as the Pilot Batch, and we also continued to pump out more pilot batches as we set our sights on brewing our first commercial release.

We brewed five more pilots including a 9% Belgian Dark Ale, a Funky Belgian Ale, a Black IPA, a Pale Ale, and a Saison. These would all go on to become commercial releases in various forms and getting them out early was huge. It gave us a lot of opportunity to test various recipes.

Our Beach House Saison, for example was brewed three times before we agreed on the final version. It also showed people we could do more than one beer and gave us some interesting content to post on social media. We gave out these batches to family and friends and drank it ourselves as we started to think about our core range.

For now, though, our priority was getting out a commercial version of the Eggnog Stout.

Contract brewing

We started talking to breweries as we looked at our options for doing our first commercial batch as a contract brew.

The way contract brewing works is that we brew the beer at someone else's venue and pay them a fixed fee to do it. The rest is up to us, from marketing and selling to putting up the money for the batch.

In the startup world, there's a thing called a Minimum Viable Product (MVP). The idea is you do the simplest and cheapest product possible to test your hypothesis for the business. When we first started, we simply wanted to test if we could make the Eggnog Stout work, so the pilot batch represented the MVP for that idea. After we knew it worked, we needed an MVP for selling it commercially. We weren't about to build a brewery: we didn't even know if we could sell the beer yet.

So contract brewing our first commercial release was an MVP of sorts. It meant we didn't have to have our own brewery, but we could do a small run of beers and test the market before investing any more time and money.

We discovered that all we needed was a producer wholesaler licence (around $1,500 and a few months of form-filling), and a brewery willing to give us a shot. There are a few things to think about when you are choosing who to contract brew with:

- Availability - Not every brewery will let people contract brew, and even if they do, they may not have tank space available. Through our time as contract brewers, we brewed at four different locations, but early on, it wasn't easy to get tank space. Once we'd forged more relationships and credibility, it became much easier.
- The brewer - You want to brew with someone you like and who knows what they are doing.
- The size - A huge system is great, but you have to sell the beer, and because you are paying to rent it, small batch contract brewing is rarely a profitable exercise. We were prepared to break even or even lose money on some brews because the purpose was market testing, not money making. For our first batch, we just wanted to crank out a few kegs, so we targeted a system around 500 to 1,000 litres.
- The facility - Not all breweries are created equal, so we investigated our options before deciding on the one to go with.
- The location - Being known as Gold Coast brewers was important to us, so we wanted a brewing location somewhere fairly close by. Transporting the finished kegs was another consideration.
- Supporting services - The brewery might also help with other requirements like off-site storage and keg hire. There is a lot to think about when you make beer, so weigh all of this up.
- Price - Of course, the price matters too.

For our first commercial batch, we decided on Beard and Brau Brewery in Tamborine Village. Chris, and his wife Tanya, welcomed the idea after a visit and a quick meeting. Chris had been brewing for years, and we'd all had his beers before. He has a small brewery (a 400-litre system and 800-litre fermenters), that made for a perfect start to our first commercial contract brew. If all went to plan, we'd be able to do a double batch and release about 14 kegs of Eggnog Stout. It was about an hour from our house and still close enough to be considered the Gold Coast.

Planning the beer

There is a lot that has to happen between planning a beer and the brew day. This is particularly true for a one-off beer in a new venue that isn't close by your house. Here is a quick rundown of how the process worked:

- Contract - It took us a long time to iron out all of the details of the contract, but we got there in the end. In hindsight, we probably should have done less on email and more in person. Plus, given it was our first beer there, we accepted that it would take a bit of back and forth.
- Scaling the recipe - It's not quite as simple as multiplying everything to get from 20 litres to 800 litres. We had a lot of discussions between us and Chris to get everything right. We had to change some ingredients and make adjustments to brew on a larger system.
- Ordering ingredients - While Chris was able to acquire the basic ingredients, it was up to us to source the yeast and the special ingredients for the Eggnog Stout, which included French brandy, spices, and Madagascan vanilla. This was pretty daunting, particularly the vanilla and the brandy, which can really add up on a brew of this size.
- Planning - There were a whole range of factors to consider around the timing for milling, brewing, adding spices, and

kegging. There were a lot of visits to the brewery, and we cut it pretty fine to keep our launch date of November 2, 2014.

- Licensing - There is also a lot of effort that goes into getting a producer wholesale licence. It's mainly procedural and involved a bunch of forms, emails, and a visit to our local council member to get Eddie's house approved as our licenced area.
- Excise and logistics - We had to consider alcohol excise duty and how we went about storing and delivering the kegs. In the end, we decided to use Beard and Brau's kegs, and we delivered the kegs ourselves. We were pretty confident we'd sell them all and that they'd get emptied quickly.
- Clothing - Chris insisted on steel cap boots... and Hawaiian shirts! Ed was on shopping duty and scored some boots for $18 and shirts for $5.
- Pricing - We also had to think about how we would price the kegs. We ended up deciding on $320 + GST. This was at the higher end for a keg of beer, particularly when compared with bigger breweries, but for a one-off batch like this, we didn't really need to beat them on price; we just didn't want to be too over the top. At this price, we would more or less break even on the batch if we sold all of the kegs.

All in all, it was a lot of thinking, talking, and emailing prior to getting started.

Yeast preparation

One of the other challenges with brewing beer at a venue other than your own is yeast preparation. We decided to do the yeast preparation ourselves. It was a big decision because it meant that we would wear more of the risk if it didn't work out. But this is what Govs was most comfortable with, so we went about getting the yeast ready a week before brew day.

Govs propagated the yeast starter from a packet of Wyeast Irish Ale strain in his spare room using an Erlenmeyer flask, fresh wort, and a stirring plate. This was grown up over three-days to the required cell count, and by the time brew day came around, we had a couple of 20-litre kegs of fresh yeast ready to go.

We didn't have a microscope at the time, so we couldn't take a yeast count on the day.

Milling the grain

We headed out on October 5th, the day before brew day, to mill the grain. There were two reasons for doing it the day before:

1. The mill Chris uses is quite small, so it took two or three hours to mill all of the grain. We wouldn't have had enough time to mill and brew on the same day.
2. The milling creates a fair bit of dust, and he wanted to have a nice clean brewery for brew day.

The milling went well, although it took a long time. Having used much bigger mills before, it was hard to spend hours on something we knew we could have done in minutes. It did teach us a good lesson. When we got our equipment, we made sure that we got a mill that would do a good job in a reasonable amount of time.

For our first brew, this was fine, and there were no issues doing the milling. We were pumped to come back at 6:00 a.m. the next day and start brewing.

Brew day

We headed up the mountain at 6:00 a.m. on Monday, October 6th for the brew day.

Chris has a rule that if you are going to work all day, you might as well pretend you are on holidays, so Hawaiian shirts were compulsory.

Lou from Stone & Wood joined us for moral support but didn't get the memo about the shirts—or she chose to ignore it, I'm not sure. But she did bring us vegan ham and cheese sandwiches courtesy of Chris and Tanya.

We loaded the mash tun with the first batch of grain and the water as well as salts and minerals to achieve the appropriate hardness and pH for the style, and we began the process of filling it with the pre-heated water.

We took turns stirring every 15 minutes or so, and Chris added the yeast that Govs had prepared to the fermenter.

We then transferred the mash to the kettle (sparging) and added the hops (Cascade and East Kent Goldings). You can find the full recipe up on the book resources page at blackhops.com.au/book.

We then emptied the spent grain using a "sophisticated" system of wheelie bins and a metal sign, which was surprisingly effective.

After the boil, we transferred the beer to the fermenter via the heat exchanger, which cooled the beer while heating the water for the second 400-litre batch. Clever stuff. It meant we had to wait for the boil before we could do the second mash, but it saved a lot of water.

We then repeated the whole process to get the full 800 litres of beer in the fermenter.

As the sun set over the back of the farm, we were all stoked to have completed our first full brew and were well and truly ready for a beer!

Why u no ferment?

All had gone more or less to plan and the fermentation had kicked off on schedule. I was actually overseas at the time when Eddie messaged me to let me know there was a bit of a problem. Apparently the beer had stopped fermenting.

This was our worst nightmare. Govs remained relatively calm, but Eddie and I didn't know a whole lot about beer at the time, and it seemed to us that the whole thing was falling apart. Not only would we lose our few thousand dollars we put into the batch, but our reputation and brand along with it.

Govs headed out to Beard and Brau and chatted with Chris and agreed to pitch some more yeast to kick the fermentation off again. In the end, it worked and came in more or less where we expected it—at around 5%.

There are a lot of variables in brewing, but as Govs said, "Beer just wants to be brewed." Things can go wrong, but they are often fixable. Fermentation stalling isn't that uncommon, and it was pretty easily fixed.

Relieved, we pushed on with the remaining tasks prior to launch.

Post brew day

There was still a lot of work to do before the launch. We had to organize the location, which ended up being HooHa Bar in South Brisbane. Those guys were awesome and very flexible with our dates. They made up a poster and started promoting the event. We still have the poster on our cellar door wall.

We also had to go back to the brewery for a few things including adding our spices at the end of fermentation and kegging the beer on completion. Because it was our first beer, we spiced it gradually to make sure we didn't overdo it.

The plan for this beer was always to make it a smashable Irish Stout with eggnog characteristics. We didn't want it to be sickly sweet, and we wanted to make sure it tasted like a nice stout at the end of the day.

Once the beer was kegged, we were ready to go. We threw together some tap decals and delivered the first keg to HooHa Bar on Sunday, hours before our launch party.

Customers

Of course, someone had to buy the beer and through a combination of getting a bit of attention in the community and Eddie busily heading out to the bars in Brisbane, we managed to sign up some amazing venues. All of these venues had agreed to take kegs before the brew was even done, and we pre-sold all of the beer quite easily.

We met with most of the bars personally, and some had tried the bottled pilot batch of the beer. All of these bars were in Brisbane except for our local craft beer bar down on the Gold Coast, Ze Pickle. Interestingly, Ze Pickle were one of only a few bars selling local small batch craft beer at the time on the Gold Coast. When we opened our brewery in 2016, we were selling most of our beer to bars on the Gold Coast.

At the time of the first commercial beer, we also had some interest from interstate, but we didn't really have enough to go around. We set up a list on our email software for interested venues and started contacting them later on when we were in a position to supply interstate.

Launch

Our launch happened on November 2nd at HooHa Bar in Southbank. It was a celebration of local Queensland craft beer with Beard and Brau, Brewtal, and Croft Brewing all putting on beers for the event.

There were nearly 70 of our friends and family there, and we drained the first 50-litre keg of Eggnog Stout in 2 hours and 20 minutes. Their previous record for draining a keg was 24 hours, so we were well stoked. It was particularly cool to see some of our mates, who were used to drinking Corona, enjoying an Eggnog Stout in the middle of summer!

Brewing our first commercial release was a huge step, and it gave us a lot of confidence to keep pushing on with our journey.

CHAPTER 5

RELATIONSHIPS

I mentioned before that it wouldn't be possible to start a business in this industry without being very good at cultivating relationships. This is something we've actively done since before we'd even thought of opening our own brewery. Once we did decide to turn it into a business, this became a prime focus for us.

Here are the main groups of people we've actively built relationships with from day one.

Local bars and restaurants

We're lucky our local craft beer industry is full of legends, so getting to know the players wasn't a big challenge for us. As we learned from The Simpsons, "You don't win friends with salad," but we can confirm you can make great friends over a beer.

When we started out, we relied heavily on some of the friendships we'd made along our journey. Whether it was checking out a new bar, trying a new beer that just got tapped, or grabbing an old favourite, we were a constant presence in the local scene. We started sharing actively on social media, particularly Instagram. Doing this regularly, we got to know many of the local bar owners, bloggers, and characters on the same mission as us.

This has been a big focus for Eddie. Ever since that first meeting with Darren 250, he worked on making friends in the craft beer industry, particularly with venues.

There's a nice story about the Great Northern Hotel in Melbourne and their distaste for alcohol reps, wine in this case. The owner disliked the wine reps so much that he had a plan for when they called to arrange meetings. He had a dog called Billy on site, and when the reps arranged a meeting, they'd come in asking for Billy, and he'd bring out the dog!

Some of these bars are very hard to get into, and they are heavily driven by relationships. No one wants to buy beer from a wanker.

When we released our first beer in November 2014, we had 14 kegs to sell, and we had bugger-all storage options, so we needed to move them quickly. This was a daunting task, which mainly fell into Eddie's lap, and he'd never really sold anything before. Walking into a bar and asking someone to buy something is not something that came naturally to him. It felt awkward, so our approach to sales has always been to make sure bars have heard of Black Hops and also know us personally. If that happens, we found the beer often sells itself. For our first batch, we started putting out a lot of content about what we were doing on our blog and social media and others were noticing too.

Eddie had been hanging out in bars regularly, and people started asking him about the Eggnog Stout. This wasn't something that happened in one day; it unfolded over months of hanging out and keeping people in the loop about how we were going with the brew.

Eddie used to do the commute from Gold Coast to Brisbane daily on the train, so naturally, HooHa Bar near the South Bank train station was a place he'd often drop into for a beer. This was probably the first bar that Eddie built up a good relationship with, and when it came to launching our commercial release, they were the first bar to come to mind to hold the launch party.

This was more or less how we sold the first batch of beer—bar by bar. Eddie would drop into bars that would ask about our progress, and we'd put a keg aside for them. We weren't 100% sure how many kegs we would get from the batch, but we pre-sold as many as possible.

Eddie's approach was very organic. He came from sitting in front of a computer, working in an office, with nothing to do with sales. He had no idea when and how bar owners wanted to be approached. But gradually, as he built relationships, the sales started to come, and there was no one best way to do it. Some sold in person, some via Facebook, some by text message, some on the phone, some via email. As time went on, we gradually built up relationships with bars in Brisbane, the Gold Coast, and interstate, along with social media contacts and an email list.

We started doing events wherever possible like Brewsvegas and Good Beer Week and The Great Australasian Beer SpecTAPular (GABS) in Melbourne. The bar scene on the Gold Coast was exploding, and we'd go to the openings and make sure we had a regular presence. This led to more great friendships and more beer sales.

By the time we opened, we were selling enough contract-brewed beer on the Gold Coast to give us confidence we would cover costs in the new brewery.

Bloggers and journalists

Darren wasn't the only blogger to write about Black Hops early on. We were actively blogging ourselves and also building relationships with other bloggers and journalists.

Judd from Brewed Crude & Bitter was one of the first to cover us with a classic review of our story titled, "The Least Covert Operation in History." We loved it so much that we sent him a t-shirt and asked if we could use the slogan, which we modified to "The Least Covert Operation in Brewing."

We also had James Smith from The Crafty Pint write an article about us, which was awesome. At the time, we'd never met the man behind the site, but that made it even better. We've since met him, and he's yet another example of this industry being full of dead set legends. We've become friends and helped out with a bunch of his events, and he's covered us quite a bit.

We followed all of the main beer blogs and connected on social media. We also embraced the traditional press because we knew that any attention helped with building a business. We put together proper press releases and professional photos to make their job easier and we reached out to them when we had newsworthy content. As it turned out we had a lot of newsworthy content prior to launching. We'll dig into that a bit more in the Marketing section.

Hop farmers and grain producers

One of the main things we learned from doing events and becoming friends with the bigger brewers was the importance of suppliers, in particular hop suppliers. Growing hops is not an easy job and it's not uncommon for entire crops to be wiped out suddenly. If specific hops are needed for your beer, you need to have a plan for making sure you can get them.

The larger breweries have hop contracts that go out five and six years, and even small amounts of certain hops were hard for us to come by early on. We deliberately didn't have any beer that relied heavily on one hop and we had to chop and change them quite a bit.

As we got closer to opening a physical location, we began talking to the suppliers about small hop contracts and started working on these relationships more and more. Grain suppliers were the same. We'd been chatting with them for months leading up to our launch and taken every opportunity to hang out and do events with them.

Grain wasn't as hard to come by, and there were a few suppliers, so it wasn't as big of a problem, but making grain isn't an easy process, so having good relationships in this field is a must.

Local farmers and producers

We also got to know local farmers, and it was surprising how often those relationships were useful. We had people lined up to take our spent grain before we were open. We worked with local farmers on food and beer events and for produce for speciality beers. Our 2016 GABS beer had 60 kilograms of fruit from local producers, and we did events with cheesemakers and local meat smokers.

The beer scene is tied heavily to the movement towards supporting locally-produced food, so building relationships with these guys was a big help.

Neighbours

Once we decided on a location for the brewery, we made an effort to become friends with our neighbours, both businesses and people living in the area. For businesses, we'd hang out at the local cafes a bit and chat to them about what they were up to. For neighbours, it meant organising meetings to discuss our plans and generally trying to be a good neighbour.

Our brewery is on a street with residential houses, so we knew that this would be important from the start. It's an ongoing challenge; you obviously can't make everyone happy, but we are always conscious of what the neighbours are thinking and feeling, and we made some concessions, such as shorter trading times and a smaller cellar door. We will delve into this a bit more later on.

Other startups and business owners

We have also been very active with other business owners and business groups. We've presented at countless events during beer festivals and attended and spoken to business groups. We've always been generous with our time and have taken every opportunity to join in events that promote other people starting businesses in our space.

We get requests a lot for this now, and we can't do all of them, but where there is a good fit, we always try to make it along. This goes a long way toward creating a great reputation in your community and should continue regardless of the size of the business.

Homebrewers

We also built a close relationship with the local homebrewing community. Often, the people wanting to attend the business events and follow in our footsteps come from the homebrew groups, so we'll do anything to help. This could be judging their awards, sampling their beers, attending their meetups, or just catching up talking beer and comparing recipes.

These guys are always supportive and represent a good grass-roots part of the beer community, so helping them out is the way to go.

Other breweries

We tried very hard to be supportive of other breweries. Again, it's a great community, and the craft beer crew and other breweries have become great friends. From very early on, we always made sure to visit other breweries when travelling and do collab brews when we had the chance. As we got settled at our own venue, we were always very supportive of other brewers coming and checking it out, especially if they brought samples!

You never know where these relationships will lead, and you don't want to become an outcast in such a tight community. Anything you can do to help and support other breweries is a good idea. Some people see this as a challenge because you know that at some level you are competing with them, but that's not how we look at it. The market is big enough for all of us, and it's our job to make sure we are relevant enough to beer buyers. Our competitors push us further, and we do the same to them, and together we gradually take over more of the market from the big brewers. As long as you have a strong point of difference, there should be no reason to fear other breweries.

An ongoing job

Being a good relationship manager and community member is an ongoing job for everyone involved in the business. It's not as simple as sucking up when you need help and then becoming insular when other people need help.

We are very grateful for the support we got when starting and believe other people deserve the same. Keep relationship building on the top of your list for the life of your business, and don't miss an opportunity to help out someone in the beer scene.

CHAPTER 6

BUSINESS MODELS

There are a lot of ways to go about creating a brewing business. All of them have their pros and cons, so it's a matter of figuring out what is right for you in your situation. We considered all of these options before arriving at our final plan.

Contract brewing

Contract brewing is something that works from a small scale level of 50-litre batches all the way to a large scale level of 10,000-litre-plus batches.

It was perfect for us when we started out. After our first brew with Beard and Brau, we started brewing small 50-litre batches at Bacchus Brewing in Brisbane. Their facility enabled us to brew 5 different 50-litre brews at once, which meant we could test out a lot of different styles.

But being a small scale brewery, it wasn't the most efficient way to make a lot of beer, which also made it comparatively expensive. We had to charge customers more than we liked and even then we weren't making any money on the beer. It was a great fit for us starting out and trying to make a name for ourselves, but it wasn't really going to take us to the next step.

There are larger options available, like Brew Pack in Sydney, who work with breweries who have outgrown their own facilities, brewing 5,000 litres per batch.

This would have been too much of a gap for us to do regularly and the idea of travelling to Sydney to brew wasn't appealing for us either.

We also had a few in-between options like Four Hearts Brewing at Ipswich where we worked with Wade Curtis on 1,200-litre batches.

There's really no reason why we couldn't have continued contract brewing indefinitely and scaled it up gradually. It would have been hard for us to make money, but perhaps not impossible.

There is a bit of discussion about whether this approach is truly "craft," given you aren't really making the beer on-site yourself. However, there's an equally compelling argument that there's not much point investing all of the money and resources into a brewery when you can use the facilities of one that already exists.

We wanted our own space. We wanted full control of the process, and we wanted our own home to show off to the Gold Coast.

Contract brewing is still an option for us as our space is limited, so if we want to do larger runs of packaged products, like cans, we will have no issue looking at contract brewing again. Our attention, however, quickly turned to figuring out how to have our own presence on the Gold Coast.

Full-scale production brewery

At the top of the spectrum is a full-scale production brewery. Something that is a decent scale like Burleigh Brewing, who have a 5,000-litre brewery and ample space for rows of 10,000-litre tanks, or Stone & Wood, who took over an old Bunnings Warehouse and have two 5,000-litre brewhouses and an outdoor section with 40,000-litre fermenters.

These guys brew, bottle, and package on-site and don't really have to go off-site for anything.

Something like this requires a lot of investment, and for us to go from a few contract brewed kegs to a multimillion dollar production brewery would have been a bit of a stretch.

You would want to be pretty confident you could sell enough beer to pull this off, and you'd also need investors who were equally confident to put up the money.

This kind of setup exists mainly to handle the end-to-end process of brewing and distributing shitloads of beer. Some will have an on-site bar but often it will be purely production.

Brewpub

A brewpub is a pub and restaurant with an on-site brewery. Generally, the breweries will be small (up to 1,000 litres is common), but they exist mainly to serve the local area. Because they can charge retail prices and do food, they can be quite profitable.

Operating a full-production brewery requires you to move a lot of beer because the margins on kegs are low. A brewpub means you can generate revenue from higher-margin items like food and soft drinks but still brew your own beer on-site.

It's a nice middle option, but brewpubs can also be very expensive to build because you are looking at a full restaurant fitout as well commissioning a brewery.

In our area, brewpubs were popping up all all over, Newstead, Catchment, Brisbane Brewing Co, Fortitude Brewing, and Four Hearts Brewing, to name a few.

If you have the capacity to run a restaurant and a pub and the desire to make beer on-site, this is the way to go.

Getting a licence is challenging and most areas require full hotel licences, which are hard to come by, and finding a location in a good spot big enough to fit a brewery is tough.

But there's no better way to give your local area the full craft beer and food experience, and this is a great way to go if your team can pull it off.

Bars

If you don't have a good reason to brew on-site, you could potentially just open a bar. If your local area has small bar licences or reasonably flexible restaurant licences, it might be a lot easier. If you can contract brew off-site, then there's a good argument for not having a brewery on-site.

Bars are a pretty fickle business, and you are a bit limited with growth when you open a local bar. They are super competitive, and staying on-trend is an ongoing challenge.

If you feel like your team could pull this off, it might be worth considering. For us, I was never too keen to open a bar, but once we build the brand more, it's something we may consider. If we wanted to expand interstate, for example, it might not make sense to invest in a whole new brewery if we are happy with our current facilities.

Brewery and cellar door

For us, the brewery and cellar door/tasting room was the option that stood out as the best fit. Breweries like this tend to be smaller (1,000 to 2,500 litres), but big enough to run profitably as a wholesale operation. Having a tasting room on-site means you can access higher-margin sales of beer over the counter as well as take-aways and growlers.

For us, it was also about establishing a local presence on the Gold Coast and giving them a taste of what other cities have: a brewery and tasting room in a convenient location close to local cafes, bars, and restaurants. It means we can be included in brewery tours and do local corporate tours and be a real part of the local food and beer scene.

It's also a potential stepping stone. It means we could open for a few hundred thousand dollars as opposed to a few million dollars. If we outgrow it, we will be at a stage where we have enough beer out there with a well-established brand, so building something bigger won't feel unachievable.

With regards to licences and regulations, the brewery and cellar door option is pretty simple in comparison to something like a brewpub. If you are only selling your own beer, you don't need any additional licences, at least in our region, to sell it over the counter direct to customers. Industrial facilities tend to be a lot cheaper than retail facilities like a bar, so you can access retail margins without the additional risk.

Online only

We've seen a few online-only brewing companies open lately, which presents another unique option. Without any physical presence, the overheads would be lower, and if you could contract brew, you'd have very little risk.

Distributing beer is a big challenge and a big expense, particularly in Australia, so you would have to carefully look at whether or not you could be profitable. You also wouldn't get any of the benefits of having a local presence in your community, which was a big part of what we were about.

For us, the decision was pretty easy, and as we grow, we will constantly look at the options to work out where to go next.

CHAPTER 7

MARKETING

In chapter two, we talked about how to build a brand. Branding and marketing work hand in hand, but marketing deserves its own chapter. It probably deserves its own book, it's so important!

Building a brand is about creating something that you stand for, cultivating your story, and presenting it in an appealing and consistent way. Marketing is about getting attention for your brand.

There are literally a million ways to do it:

- Some brands will go very hard on marketing, post regularly, take out big ads, always keep up a presence.
- Others can get by with a great product and a cult following.
- Some will spend up big on traditional paid channels.
- Others will focus on more organic channels.

It's a good idea to aspire to be a company that doesn't ever have to do any marketing, but in reality, it's very rare for companies to not have to market themselves in some way. You have to be honest about where you are at and what you are good at.

It's about finding a killer growth channel, or a few of them, and focusing hard on those.

Finding your killer growth channels

By observing a lot of successful entrepreneurs, I've noticed new businesses that do well tend to market themselves in only one or two ways. Some are experts at face-to-face sales, some are great copywriters, some blow up on social media, others focus on customer experience and product. Generally, when businesses try to launch with multiple channels, it results in them mastering none of them.

Here are some questions that will help you find your one or two killer growth channels:

1. Traction - How did your current audience hear about you? This will help you work out what has been effective.
2. Founders - What are the unique skills of the founding team? This can give you an enormous advantage over any competitors who have no marketing experts on the founding team.
3. Trends - What are some up and coming trends you can jump on? In our case, Instagram was exploding, and we doubled down on it.
4. Differentiation - What is no one else doing? You will stand out much more and market much cheaper if you can find a channel that isn't being well utilised.

Choose one or two channels and do your best to do marketing on those channels as well, if not better, than anyone else in the space. Then pay attention to what is gaining traction.

Content marketing

In our case, we chose content marketing because it met all of our criteria. Content marketing is putting out information like blog posts and podcasts in order to build a high-ranking website and a social media following. It's about telling your story and being as useful as possible in order to get free attention and build trust. It's the polar opposite to taking out paid ads in the Yellow Pages or on TV.

Here are a few practical ways it works:

- We write practical blog posts on how to build a "craft beer brewery." We make them as useful as we can, people share them on social media, other blogs link to us, and that makes us rank better in Google. When people look for a brewery on the Gold Coast, we are at, or close to, the top of the front page, despite some of our competitors being around for many years.
- We put out useful information on a podcast, so when we go to events, people feel like they know, like, and trust us already. This breaks the ice, and it leads to customers, partnerships and much more.
- We put photos on Instagram using some relevant beer-related hashtags. Because we share good content, other Instagrammers notice us and re-share our stuff and we build an audience on that platform. People are used to seeing our brand, and when they go to a bar that has us on tap, they will be more likely to try our beer.
- We present at business events and help people start their own businesses. This helps us build relationships with event organizers that lead to private tastings, event sponsorships, and additional social media sharing in the business community.

- All of the content we share builds our authority in the industry and gets the attention of local journalists. When given the opportunity, we tell our story to the press and try to get attention for key projects. This makes the readers of the papers feel part of our story and more likely to drink our beer or come into the brewery.

The list goes on. Any time we put out any image, article, blog post, or event presentation, we are doing content marketing.

Here's how content marketing measured up against our four criteria for a killer growth channel:

1. Traction - We noticed from the small amount of blog posts we had done that we were starting to get serious traction. We were mentioned on blogs, press were covering us, and people would often tell us at events how much they enjoyed the content.
2. Founders - I had built a decent business already using content marketing and was speaking internationally on the topic. I had just launched my second book, *Content Machine*, which was a #1 best seller on Amazon. We were all keen on the idea, and open minded when it came to marketing and very active online.
3. Trends - I noticed businesses popping up that were built purely through marketing on social media, often solely Instagram. Instagram was exploding, and most people were using it to post pictures of their breakfast. A lot of people didn't realize the power of the platform and other emerging networks like Snapchat for building a business.
4. Differentiation - The biggest thing for us is that we noticed that most other breweries weren't doing content marketing. I came from the online marketing world

where this is second nature, but in the more traditional world of brewing, the idea of releasing a whole bunch of secrets and useful information to help others was relatively different.

Our content ended up becoming a huge asset for us. Our investors became aware of us through the content, and we got customers, collaborators, press contacts, and much more just through the blog posts. We were asked to speak at events, written about in the paper, and developed a solid following.

The content helped us outrank most of our competitors in Google before we even opened the brewery. It also provided us with ongoing content for social media.

Understanding the basics of content marketing

Here are some of the fundamentals of how we think about Content Marketing:

1. Content marketing is not about promotion, it's a fundamentally different way to market a business. If we filled our site with articles about how good our beer was, or filled our Instagram with professional product shots, it wouldn't work. Content marketing is about serving our audience and earning their attention and trust. If we can do a good job at serving them, then ultimately we will build our brand and it will work to our benefit.
2. Quality is more important than quantity. There's no point putting out hundreds of social media posts, articles, or podcasts if they aren't any good. Work out what represents quality content for your audience and do that. In my 10 years of doing it, I've put out thousands, if not tens of

thousands, of pieces of content. Most of it went unnoticed; only the great stuff works.

3. Your audience determines the quality of your content. Get to know exactly who loves your content and live to serve them. If your audience loves your Instagram posts, then that is quality to them. If they love your stories, then do more of that. In our case, we learned that they love detailed blog posts about our journey and our podcast, *Operation Brewery*. This is where we focused our attention because we could see it was getting traction.

4. Put out content that is related to your business. It's okay to be broad with your content, but if you want to build a brand around brewing, then the content has to be about beer in some way. In our case, things like recipes, procedures on how to make tap decals and jockey boxes, and podcast episodes about how we chose our location or how we got funding were the ones that people liked. All of the content is about beer or brewing in some way, so our audience became homebrewers, bar owners, brewers and drinkers. In other words, they were potential customers and partners.

5. Take every opportunity to build an online audience. Building an email list on our blog for example, or building a list doing the Pozible campaign or building followers on Instagram or Facebook. If there are things we can do to make our audience bigger, we will do them. Collaborating with other people who have a good social media following is one obvious way.

6. It's not good enough to be better, you have to be different. Our content only works because there aren't thousands of other people doing it. If you want to capture people's attention, you need to do something different. This goes for business in general and any form of marketing including content marketing.

7. It helps if there is an underlying vision or belief behind what you do. In our case, our belief was that it should be easy for keen brewers and others in the industry to find information on everything they need to get into the craft beer scene in Australia. Currently, it's difficult. There are too many secrets and too many companies living in the dark ages. It's time for the trends of transparency and freedom of information to hit the beer scene. With this vision in mind, it became easy to think about the sorts of content to put out. This fit well with our slogan, "The Least Covert Operation in Brewing," and we made an effort to be as transparent as possible.

8. Don't follow the competition; you will never be able to replicate someone else's success. Just look at what you are doing and do more of what is working. Get inspiration from others, but don't assume that what works for them will work for you.

9. Be as generous as possible. We give out every detail of what we do, including the people we work with, the materials and ingredients we use, our suppliers for equipment, and much more. This is what the audience wants, and the more generous we can be, the more our audience will like and trust us.

10. Always be telling a story. James Smith from The Crafty Pint once told me, "You have given us more reasons to write about you than any other new brewery I can think of." This is because we are actively looking for opportunities to tell stories. When we launched our first commercial beer just weeks after doing our first homebrew, that was a story. Every collab brew we did was a story. When we brewed a beer with sponge cake in it, that was a story. When we hit our crowdfunding target in one day, that was a story. Great stories make great content, and if you want to get other people talking about you, writing about you,

linking to you, or sharing your content on social media, you have to tell great stories.

11. Work to your strengths. No one can be great at everything, so we do what we are good at. I do the writing, Govs does the talking, and Eddie does the Instagram pics. Every few weeks, we all get together and do the podcast. If you aren't a good writer, you might not want to write blog posts. If you aren't good at video, then stay away from that. Just try to find something that your audience likes and that you or someone on your team is good at.

12. Content marketing is the new Search Engine Optimisation (SEO). In the past, business owners had no clue how Google worked, so they paid thousands of dollars to SEO consultants to try to outsmart Google. These days, we know exactly what Google wants—loads of high quality content. We can skip the dodgy SEO tactics and get straight to doing what Google wants. I've found time and again, across multiple businesses, that this works far better than anything else to boost your rankings in Google.

Once you understand what your audience wants, you can get better and better at delivering great content in whatever ways you deliver it. For example:

- Eddie noticed people love pictures of tanks on Instagram, so you'll see regular pics of our brewery on our @blackhopsbeer account.
- Govs noticed people love hearing our stories at events, so when he delivers talks, he always focuses in on the interesting parts of our story.
- I noticed going to events that people love the podcast, so we put out regular episodes leading up to our launch and then continued it after launch.

- We also noticed that people loved the written articles on our site about our story of building the brewery. That's why this book exists. It's just a form of content marketing that has grown from the articles on the site.

Here are some specific ways we've used content marketing to get attention for Black Hops.

Blog posts

Very early on, we set up WordPress and started writing blog posts on our site, things like:

- Telling key parts of our story, such as how we brewed our first homebrew batch and first commercial release.
- Writing long instructional articles on things such as putting together budget tap decals and keg collars and how to build a portable beer-serving jockey box on a budget.
- Breaking down our decisions around ordering and inspecting our brewery equipment in China.
- Releasing the pitch deck we used to secure our investment money.

Any time we felt like we had something useful to say, we wrote about it in an article. Those blog posts got traffic to the site, linked to by other sites, and shared on social media. As a result, people saw our brand regularly and our site authority rose.

By the time we launched, we'd written 33 articles on the blog, and we were getting around 4,000 visits to the site each month. We had 600 backlinks to the site and were ranking for most of the beer-related keywords in our area.

This is a nice start, but it's by no means putting us on top of established websites in the industry. Building site authority and a social media audience takes a long time, and incumbents have a massive advantage, but if there is anything you can do to make the process quicker, you should try to do it!

Operation Brewery podcast

We noticed that no other brewery had a podcast. There were other beer podcasts, but we figured people would want to get the inside view of what it's like to start a brewery. We committed to doing a 10-part series called Operation Brewery.

We brainstormed the various topics we could talk about from getting investment dollars to launching a crowdfunding campaign to ordering equipment to choosing a location. Then we set up our podcast on our site and in iTunes, and we started recording episodes.

It's not obvious when a podcast is going well because it doesn't boost your site traffic very much, and it's not the kind of thing people often share on social media. We noticed the impact of it when we started attending in-person events and talking to other people in the industry and were blown away by the people who listened to the podcast. At every event we'd do, we'd have a handful of people come up and tell us that they loved it! This kept us going and also convinced us to keep going after the original 10-part series.

When we launched our brewery, we had around 250 podcast subscribers and close to 10,000 total downloads or around 1,000 listens per episode.

Again it's not huge numbers, but it's the sort of content that builds a lot of trust. People feel like they know us and they trust us when they listen to it, and it's a great brand builder.

Email list

We recognized the power of an email list early on. We also realized that it wasn't something that other companies were doing in a very sophisticated way. I'd been a regular customer of lots of other breweries, and I'd never had an email from them.

In the online marketing world, it's recognised that "the money is in the list," so we made an effort to build our email list from day one.

We had email lists for venues, opt-in forms for people wanting to get our content, and a list of people who backed the Pozible campaign.

When we opened, we also had a connection between people who signed up to our loyalty program and our email list in MailChimp, so we could continue to grow the list.

By the time we launched, we had a list of over 500 people. Again, those are not huge numbers, but a list of 500 people who know you and trust you, who you can contact any time you need to send out a message, is a nice asset.

Email has been forgotten by a lot of new businesses because of the prevalence of social media, but with an email list, you have 100% control of the asset and you get direct one-on-one communication with your people. A 500-person email list is worth a lot more than 500 likes or followers on social media that can become worthless overnight when the platform dies off or they change the rules and make you pay to promote to them.

Social media

Social media was something we took seriously even before we launched. We were all regulars on Facebook, in Facebook groups, and on Instagram. We saw it as a way to build trust and create attention in a way that was fun.

We had a genuine belief that we would be able to market our business without advertising or paying reps to sell the beer, at least early on. We did it through content and a heavy involvement in social media.

We didn't try to be everywhere, focusing primarily on Facebook and Instagram. Here are some of the things that served us well on each platform.

On Facebook

We set up our page facebook.com/blackhopsbeer very early on.

- We actively shared our content with others on our page. Our page grew from scratch to over 2,000 likes around launch time.
- We used Facebook comments on our blog, which increased sharing.
- We made the effort to format all of our content to Facebook guidelines to maximise sharing.
- We shared all of our content via our page and monitored it regularly to see what got the best reach and shares. We then aimed to do more of that type of content.

- We used Facebook Events for promoting our events (lots of great sharing).
- We actively tagged other people in the industry in our posts when relevant. They did the same, and so our name got out to a wider audience.
- We used our Facebook group when we wanted to get key messages out and needed support on something.
- We Facebook live-streamed our podcast episodes once Facebook released that feature in 2016.
- We were active in other beer-related Facebook groups to help build the community and represent our brand.
- We made an effort to respond to all comments.

On Instagram

We started our instagram account, @blackhopsbeer, as soon as we brewed our first homebrew Eggnog Stout.

- We post images multiple times daily and pay attention to what works well.
- We learned how to take high-quality photos and stopped uploading bad ones.
- We followed and actively commented and engaged with others in the industry.
- We weren't afraid to use it to promote our content like blog posts and podcast episodes.
- We learned from people who had done well on Instagram and tried to incorporate some of their ideas into our account.
- We often visited bars when our beer was on and shared pics tagging the bar and writing a useful update with a good quality picture.
- Once other people started sharing photos of our decals in bars, we re-shared those via our account.

- We started a bunch of hashtags and monitored them; #blackhops and #operationbrewery, for example.
- We always kept an eye on mentions and commented when people were shouting us out.
- We regularly updated the bio and URL in our profile to drive leads to the website.
- We kept a consistent voice by having Eddie as the main person running it.

By the time we launched, we had almost 4,000 followers, and the account was growing at 10% per month.

Snapchat

We started our snapchat account (@blackhopsbeer) properly once we opened our brewery. Before that, we didn't feel like we had enough stories to tell on there, but after launch it was easier. We cover things like:

- Live podcast recordings.
- Videos of brew days or dry hopping or anything brewing related.
- Snaps of people enjoying our beers at the cellar door.
- Any news we want to get out there.
- Videos of events or functions with venues.

We decided the easiest way to manage it was for Eddie to do Instagram and Govs to do Snapchat.

Video

We also did a small amount of video at key points throughout our journey. I'm a believer that you don't want to do video unless it's going to be good, so we used it sparingly. But we did do a few videos, which worked well for us:

- For our Pozible crowdfunding campaign, we had our mate Dave shoot a quick video re-using some elements from other videos and re-doing some in our soon-to-be-opened brewery.
- When we did work at the brewery, we captured it on time-lapse on our phone. Knocking down walls was one example, our designer drawing our logo was another, and the graffiti artist painting our wall was another. These were all well received, generally getting over 500 views on Instagram and over 1,000 views on Facebook.
- We used Facebook Live to stream podcast episodes, which turned into videos on our page, which also went surprisingly well.

If you feel that you can do video well, it's a huge opportunity. Not a lot of people do it well, and the social networks now favour video very heavily in their algorithms, which means if you can do it well, it will be pushed in front of more people.

Press

Getting press coverage is important for spreading your message and getting attention from the public, and the best part is that it's free!

Creating content, being as useful as possible, and making sure your story is out there is the best way to get the attention of press outlets. It's not the sort of thing that happens overnight the day you launch; it happens gradually as you become more and more relevant in your space.

In our case, we benefited a lot from press from the day we distributed our first homebrew to the day we opened our brewery doors.

We learnt early on from our blog and social media posts which stories had more impact and reach than others and made sure we did more like them. Typically, for us, it was the less self-serving stories like instructions for putting together jockey boxes or tap decals, or collabs with local businesses, or crazy ingredients used in certain brews.

A lot of this ended up becoming press stories in local blogs, the local paper, or even some big international publications.

The key to getting press coverage is understanding what a good story means to the audience of the publication.

For example, brewing a beer with oysters in it isn't a huge deal, but for the readers of the Gold Coast Bulletin, this is a crazy idea that deserved a full page article!

In another example, a local journalist saw us post a picture of our spent grain being taken away by a farmer. That turned into a full article in the paper the next day. To us, it wasn't a big deal. Most breweries do this and it's even written into our Development Application that we would do it. But it's a great feel-good story for the paper, so it's excellent press material.

Answering the Call of Duty

By far the biggest press opportunity came our way via an unexpected source. Calling our brewery Black Hops got us a fair bit of attention. The comparisons with the Activision game, Call of Duty® Black Ops, had crossed our minds. It is one of the biggest games on earth, and it would often come up in conversations about our name.

One day, we got an email from a media agency in Sydney. The email said that the agency was representing Activision and wanted to talk about brewing an official beer for the upcoming Call of Duty® game Black Ops III. It seemed unlikely, and on top of that, the name of the game in the email was incorrect. Eddie brought this up on one of our calls and said he thought it was spam.

I did some investigation into the company and it seemed legit, so we decided to pursue it. From then on, Govs dealt with it and it seemed like an excellent opportunity. Apparently, the agency staff were brainstorming ideas with Activision for marketing the game, and the idea of a beer came up. They had heard about us through our content and the press we'd received, so we were immediately in the picture.

For months, Govs worked back and forth with them on every detail of the beer: what we'd brew, the packaging design, the quantity, where we'd brew, and everything in between. We were adamant that the beer had to be something we were proud of. A lot of celebrity beers had been good publicity but bad beer. We insisted the beer had to be black, and then it was up to Govs to come up with something that would work for the gaming audience.

Govs brewed a black pale ale in his garage and sent bottles to Activision in Sydney as samples. The head of Activision in Australia personally tried it, loved it, and signed off.

Eddie and I weren't really convinced it was real until we had a conference call with them while we were in China inspecting our equipment!

We made plans to brew a black pale ale by contract at Brew Pack in Sydney, and were sworn to secrecy about the project. In October 2015, I flew back from Bangkok to the Gold Coast overnight and after no sleep, met Eddie and Govs at the airport bar for a beer at 6:00 a.m. We immediately flew to Sydney where we spent the entire day checking up on the beer at Brew Pack and filming the promotional video.

They had a director and a crew of five people for the video. This was when we were certain that this was actually real!

When we finally released the beer and the marketing content, it went viral, and within 48 hours of the press release, had circumnavigated the globe and onto the screens of many people who had not been exposed to much craft beer. Huge YouTube accounts and big gaming websites were "unboxing" the beer, and we had months of positive press including local newspaper and TV coverage.

For us, doing a Black Pale Ale wasn't the most aggressive beer we've done. But for gamers, it was a nice angle to have a beer that tasted like a pale ale, was delivered in a black bottle, and poured black. It was like a Black Ops covert operation.

Content marketing and press work hand in hand. If you can tell your story to your own audience, the next challenge is to work out which parts of it are appealing to a wider audience. Some of our stories were small scale, and others, like brewing a beer with the largest entertainment franchise on earth, a little bigger! It all helps to grab attention and build hype around your brand.

Pay attention to what other breweries are getting press about and weave that into your content plan. If big opportunities come up, don't just think about the financial reward, think about whether or not it's a good story and whether it can be used for large-scale, free press.

Staying on top of trends

One final point about content marketing and social media is to try to stay on top of the current trends. Things change incredibly fast. In early 2015, for example, there was no Facebook Live, Periscope and Instagram were exploding, while Snapchat was just emerging.

At the time of writing this, Instagram is maturing, Facebook Live is going very well, Snapchat is exploding, and Periscope and Twitter are becoming less relevant. This stuff literally changes in a matter of months, so make sure you have someone on your team who can stay on top of it.

Look at what other people in the industry are doing, but more importantly, look outside the industry. Everything that's happening in the beer industry with online marketing, I've seen months, if not years, earlier by following online marketing people.

Social media can't be ignored, and because it changes so rapidly, you need to be constantly on the lookout for what's next. Sometimes that means trying new things or investing time into platforms that will ultimately die off. But there's a huge benefit in being early on these platforms, so I think it's worth the risk.

CHAPTER 8

RAISING MONEY

When we first set out to build a brewery, everyone told us we would need to raise some money. They also said it would be the least of our worries. The problem was, none of us had ever been involved in a business that had raised money before. You may be in the same situation, so this chapter will help you present your idea in a way that appeals to potential investors.

In our case, we were able to get the bulk of the money required by ourselves. We needed more, though, so we looked to family and friends to fill the gap.

Family and friends as investors

We started this process by mentioning to our friends and family what we were doing and sitting down and chatting with them about the idea. We did this using a pitch deck that I outline below. If you aren't familiar with the term, it's a presentation used when talking about your business to investors (pitching).

The structure of the pitch deck gave us a good excuse to do some research and think about how we could present our idea.

In the details below, I'll break down every slide, why it was included, and how it went. You can download an editable source file of the pitchdeck at blackhops.com.au/book.

Slide one - Welcome and Slogan

"The least covert operation in brewing"

We started off with a nice image and our slogan "The Least Covert Operation in Brewing". The idea of the business being called Black Hops and us going about it in a transparent way, sharing everything we learned along the way, was a good way to start.

In your case, just add something that grabs attention and builds interest. Investors are ultimately looking for a point of difference that will help you stand out, make money, and return their investment.

Slide two - The Problem

The problem

- Queensland has very few places for craft brewers to 'contract brew' beer

- The Gold Coast has one craft beer bar and one brewery

- Both Sydney and Melbourne have established facilities that attract the best brewers

- Every other major city in Australia has a thriving and exploding craft beer bar and microbrewery scene

Most businesses are started to solve some sort of problem or take advantage of an opportunity. Investors want to know that you aren't just doing this for fun; you are actually going after a gap in the market.

For us, it was about taking advantage of the growth in the craft beer space and that the Gold Coast was yet to catch up to the other major cities.

Slide three - About Us

Enter Black Hops Brewing

In 2015 we are building Queensland's 3rd largest privately owned brewery. And we are putting the Gold Coast on the map as a craft beer destination.

We are sharing our journey and bringing the craft beer community with us.

We want you to come too.

This is where we introduce Black Hops and what we are up to. At the time, we were saying "Queensland's 3rd-largest, privately-owned brewery." By the time we launched, this wasn't the case, but it gave some idea of the opportunity. In your case, just reinforce who you are, what you are doing, and why you are doing it.

Slides four and five - Traction

Traction

- First commercial brew Eggnog stout pre-sold 14 kegs to top craft beer bars in Brisbane

- First keg sold out in 2 hours 20 minutes at our launch

- Eggnog Stout rates 4 stars on Untappd making it one of the highest rating Queensland beers

- Accepted into GABS 2015, asked to brew for Good Beer Week, Brewsvegas and others

This is one of the most important slides; it's where you can really impress your investors. Investors want to get behind something that's going well, so this is where we got into some of the traction in our brief history up until that point around beer ratings, sales, and marketing.

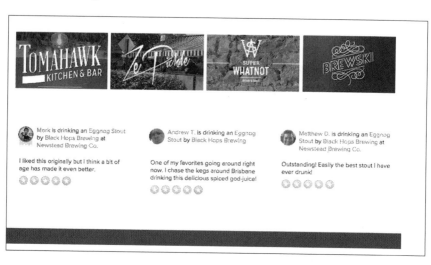

We kept that going on the next slide with some comments from other people about our first beer. It's always a good idea to not just talk about your grand plans, but to show evidence that other people are also on board. Investors love traction, and we took every opportunity to include elements of external proof of traction.

Slide six - Market Opportunity

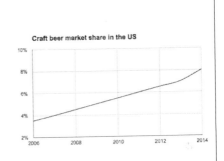

Market opportunity

- Craft beer makes up 3% of the Australian beer market

- In the US craft beer has risen from 3% to 8%

- Total Australian beer market size: $5b

- IBIS forecast 5% 5 year growth for Australian craft beer sector

Craft beer market share in the US

Of course, investors ultimately are in it to make money, so we needed to show that there was good growth potential for what we were doing. We compared the craft beer scene in Australia to the early days of the U.S. when craft beer had similar market share (3%) and showed a chart of what happened in the years after.

Obviously, we and the investors think Australia is going to follow a similar trajectory and can see it happening already.

Slide seven - Product

Product

- We make creative but approachable beer

- First beer (Eggnog Stout) surprised a few people and encouraged non stout drinkers to try something different

- We have brewed 15 pilot batches and we are ready to release a full range of beers when we open our own facility

In this slide, we spoke to the specifics of the beer we will be brewing. This included our first commercial beer but also the fact that we'd been busy brewing many pilot batches to arrive at a broader core range.

Show investors that you know what you are doing when it comes to making great beer!

Slide eight - Projected Revenue

Projected revenue

- Year 1 profit margin 6% (min capacity)

- Full capacity margin 40%, revenue $5m+

- Break up (83% kegs, 17% cellar door)

- Revenue projections are extremely conservative. Contract brewing, bottling, merchandise and cellar door events are not included

This one was a tricky one given we were in our infancy, and so we had to make some projections for revenue and start thinking about the break up of cellar door vs production beer.

Although a few things have changed since we put this presentation together, this was our best guess at the time. We initially thought we would more or less break even the first year, and we wanted to show what it would look like if we got the brewery size and location we wanted running at full capacity.

We also provided detailed projections for every year that showed what we thought we would hit as opposed to what could be our technical full capacity.

Slide nine - Marketing and Growth

Marketing and growth

- Create a great product that people love and share
- Share our journey through content (blog), social media & press
- Our story is resonating with beer lovers already
- Networking with bars and industry events

This slide is where we explained how we intended to grow the business. We feel like we have a bit of a point of difference in terms of how we are getting attention by sharing our journey and putting out content. We also talked about networking and getting out there and building a community.

We are quite keen to build our business by creating a great product, building great networks and sharing our journey, not by paying lots of money in advertising or other costs. We made this clear in the pitch, and investors were happy to hear our plans didn't involve spending shitloads on paid ads.

In your case, you need to tap into your own strategy for getting attention and growing the business. Look for any opportunity to showcase the unique skills of the founders here when it comes to marketing.

Slide 10 - Team

Dan: Built a million dollar WordPress business in under 2 years.

Award winning content marketer and online influencer.

Govs: Extremely well regarded brewer with 10 years experience.

Has brewed most of Queensland's best beers (4 out of 7 in the top 100 of 2014).

Eddie: Networking, relationships and all round legend.

Beer fanatic and friend to everyone in the Qld craft beer scene

This is the slide where we spoke about our founding team. Investors want to know their money is in safe hands and the team has a good mix of skills needed to build a business. This included a technical product person (in our case a brewer, Govs), someone with business and marketing experience (me) and someone who can form the right relationships to get the beer into bars (Eddie).

You will need a founding team if you want to get investors on board. Most of them won't believe that you can grow a good business with just one person. Your founding team members should have a mix of skills. Investors need to know you can make a great product, execute great marketing, and manage a business. Any other skills are a big bonus, but these three are essential.

Slide 11 - Competition

Competition

We will be competing with other craft breweries and big breweries for tap space in bars.

The Queensland scene has been hugely supportive, easily selling our first 14 kegs before we brewed the beer. All of our customers have asked us for more and we've had plenty of enquiries from interstate that we can't yet fulfil.

Businesses never exist in isolation, so it's useful to include a conversation about your competitors. The craft beer industry is pretty tight in Australia, and we generally see other brewers as colleagues not competitors. But we still needed to address the choices that customers have when it comes to buying beer and the choices that bars have when it comes to purchasing kegs.

On this slide, include a rundown of who you will be competing against and what you know about them and be realistic but confident.

Slide 12 - Investment

Investment

$xx0,000 total cost of setting up 2,000L operation (which includes $30k capital for cash-flow)

$xx0,000 by founders

Raising $xxx,000 for xx% of the business

It's important to have a firm idea of exactly how much you are looking for and what percentage equity you are prepared to give up for the investment. You need to go after it with confidence.

These numbers become your valuation which reflects how much the business or idea is worth to you. This will become something you negotiate, but it's a good starting point.

We felt we had a reasonably high valuation for something that didn't yet exist, but we were very confident in the idea and didn't want to shortchange ourselves. We didn't get exactly what we were after, but we weren't too far off.

We've kept the specifics out of this slide to protect the investors involved.

Slide 13 - Final slide

> "The guys have set the bar very high with Eggnog Stout so I imagine there's a rather loud buzz of expectation circling the Gold Coast right about now.
>
> Maybe it's a cluster of Blackhawk helicopters? More than likely it's those venues champing at the bit."
>
> 250beers.com.au

We finished the pitch deck off with the quote from Darren 250 who said in his article that everyone was expecting big things from us. We felt this did a nice job of capturing the excitement about what we were doing. External validation is always good, so it's not just you talking about how good you are.

Why people invest

Each slide in the pitch deck is designed to achieve something in relation to moving someone through the thought process of buying into an idea. It's a very similar process to when you yourself make any purchasing decision. Here are a few examples:

- Dealing with objections - When you make a purchasing decision, you ask yourself a lot of questions that relate specifically to concerns you have about what you are buying. For example, when you buy a new car, you think:

Is it safe?
Is it overpriced?
Is it going to be superseded in six months?

A good marketing plan will deal with these objections up front so you don't spend any time dwelling on them. When someone invests in a brewery, they have questions too:

How are these guys different?
Does the founding team have the necessary skills?
Can they actually make good beer?
Is there room in the market for another brewery?
Will the market be growing?

Think about what investors will be thinking as they review your pitch deck and address these things head on. This is so your presentation answers their questions before they ask them.

- Social proof - You are much more likely to buy something if someone you trust has bought it and likes it. It's no different with investing; the investors want to know that they aren't alone in believing in this idea. Include lots of external proof of the quality of your product, as well as any evidence that other people are on board with what you are doing (rewards, ratings, testimonials, etc).
- Design - Whether you know it or not, when you make a purchasing decision, you subconsciously pay a lot of attention to how it looks. Don't skimp on design because a poorly-designed pitch deck will show you to be an amateur, and investors will disregard it. Use high-quality images, and if you don't have strong design skills, pay a good designer to put together a nice pitch deck for you.

- Story - Everyone loves a good story. Practice telling your story, and let it flow through every slide in your presentation. We had Govs on board, and he loves to tell the Black Hops story. All he needed was the slides in the right place (where we came from, where we are now, significant milestones, where we want to go, etc), and the rest came naturally.

You can wrap your pitch up however you like, but be ready for detailed questions on all of the items covered. Investors will notice if you present the idea as something you are passionate about. They are after a financial return but they are also human, and humans don't want to miss out on being involved in an exciting opportunity.

Reward-based crowdfunding

As we got closer to opening, we ran into a few inevitable delays. In the early stages, a day or two here and there didn't feel like much. But as time went on, the bills started adding up. Once we had our location, every month we were paying out rent, forklift hire, coldroom hire, wages for the founders, electricity, power, gas, water, and more.

When we realised we were going to be cutting it fine, we had to look at other options. A chance meeting with Alan, one of the founders of a local crowdfunding platform called Pozible, led me back to the idea of doing a reward-based crowdfunding campaign.

Alan had called me about something unrelated to Black Hops, and we got to talking about the brewery. He told me we were able to sell alcohol on Pozible with the right licenses, and the alcohol campaigns were some of the most successful. This was in contrast to Kickstarter, where I'd found alcohol wasn't allowed as a reward.

On Pozible, there had been a bunch of successful campaigns, including a recent campaign for Poor Tom's Gin that had raised $69,000!

In the crowdfunding space, you can pre-sell rewards to backers (reward-based) or in some countries, sell shares in your business (equity-based). BrewDog in the UK and Yeastie Boys in New Zealand are two examples of breweries who have launched successful equity-based crowdfunding campaigns.

In Australia, however, equity-based campaigns were not legalised when we initially began our crowdfunding campaign. However, there is a good chance they will be by 2017, and so this is another option to consider.

For us, the only option we had was a reward-based campaign, which I prefer anyway because I don't like the idea of giving up equity unless you absolutely have to.

We looked into the beer-related crowdfunding campaigns more thoroughly where we found mixed results. A few bars had crowdfunded their beer taps and there had been some failed brewery launches. No one had actually launched a brewery in Australia via crowdfunding. This made us a little nervous, but also represented a good opportunity. If we could be first, that would be a good story.

We decided to go for it, and we put together a plan for running a crowdfunding campaign on Pozible. It was the start of 2016 and about the time we were hoping to open. Unfortunately, because of Council delays, we were a few months off.

We kicked the crowdfunding campaign off on January 1, 2016, with a 10-week plan involving pre-planning, campaign activities, and post-campaign tasks.

Here is a rundown of the things to think about for a crowdfunding campaign as well as the lessons we learned. You can get a copy of the exact template we used at blackhops.com.au/book.

The must-have inclusions for crowdfunding

These are the things that are absolutely essential when embarking on your crowdfunding campaign.

Plan, plan, and plan

Benjamin Franklin once said, "If you fail to plan, you are planning to fail!" In other words, you are going to need a well-thought-out plan before you kick off if you want to run a successful campaign.

Pozible have released data about their first five years of operation in which time they've hosted over 10,000 projects. It mentions the top reason for campaigns failing: not enough planning for promotional strategy.

With the Black Hops campaign, we put together a 10-week plan in Trello (a project management app) with tasks to do every week leading up to as well as during the campaign.

The plan is a public doc that I put together which you can check out at blackhops.com.au/book.

Here's the bottom line: According to Pozible, if you hit 30% of your minimum target on your first day of fundraising, then you will be almost guaranteed to hit your target. Make this the underlying focus of your crowdfunding plan.

Your target audience

Crowdfunding relies on people to give you money upfront for a product or service that can be months away from being tangible.

Think through exactly who your target market is for your campaign. I have seen quite a few failed crowdfunding campaigns and I've often thought to myself, *Why would anyone buy this?*

This is the million-dollar question you have to ask yourself. Who do you know that will buy your rewards, and why will they buy? Why is it interesting or valuable to them? Given you are aiming to hit at least 30% of your target on day one, that will probably come from people you know. If you can't visualise enough people to make up 30% of your target on day one, then I'd say there is a good chance your campaign will fail.

Like any other business transaction, it's not charity. People aren't going to give you money for nothing. There needs to be something of interest to them as well as something valuable for them to buy.

I've seen some campaigns that have no story, are poorly executed, and are completely self-serving. Don't fall into this trap because you will fail.

Have a well-designed campaign page

Whether you like it or not, design is something used by every customer to judge the validity of what businesses are selling. If it looks cheap, potential backers will assume that whatever you are making will also be cheap.

As an entrepreneur you need to understand design. With the tools provided with platforms like Pozible, you are able to create really nice looking campaign pages. In our case, we had nice photos taken and a great design for our brand, and we laid the page out neatly. That's all it took for a sweet-looking campaign page.

Create an epic video

According to research done by Indiegogo, one of the largest global crowdfunding sites, campaigns with a pitch video raise four times more funds than campaigns without one.

When we kicked off our crowdfunding campaign, we put a two-and-a-half minute professionally-produced video upfront on our campaign page. Our aim was to use storytelling to engage and educate potential supporters whilst representing our brand as genuine, likable, and professional. The video also helps with credibility, and people can see we are the real deal and not just having a laugh.

Choose the parts of your story that you think will connect with your community and focus in hard on that part of the story throughout the video. Include as much proof as you can. Images of real products and people talking about how good your product is are good examples. People want to be confident that they are backing a winner. Keep a few chopped up or edited versions of the video for sharing on social media throughout the campaign.

For our video, Activision were happy for us to reuse parts of the Call of Duty® beer video in our crowdfunding campaign video so we weaved it into our story. This gave us a lot of credibility and made the video a lot more compelling.

If you have any affiliations, be sure to highlight them in your storytelling to give credibility and weight to your campaign.

Putting a good quality video together can be expensive, so we had a professional videographer mate of ours give us a hand with it and deliver a professional end product at an affordable price. Get help from your friends if you can, but only if you know they do great work.

Set up an ambassador group

A key part of our crowdfunding strategy was setting up an ambassador group on Facebook. This helped us create an engaged audience upfront who helped us promote our campaign.

To do this, we set up a page on our site telling people about the campaign and asking for their email so that we could notify them when we went live. When people signed up for the email, we invited them to join the ambassador group on Facebook. They could help us promote the campaign and, in return, we'd make ourselves available to them to answer any questions. We'd also notify them exactly when we launched so they could scoop up the Early Bird reward.

When we launched, we notified the ambassador group first. Next we informed the people who signed up on the email opt-in page. We then put it out on social media as well as emailing our main email list.

The impact of that process was significant. The ambassador group snapped up most of the early bird offers and by the time we emailed the list, there were only a few left. Those went quickly, too, and by the time we shared it publicly, we were already into the other nine rewards. The result of this was that we hit 50% of our target in the first few hours before we even launched publicly.

Plan your rewards carefully

To plan your rewards scheme, figure out how you can offer early rewards to achieve 30% of your goal on day one.

Our early bird reward to our Facebook ambassador group was designed for this purpose.

The reward was set at $100, and we limited it to 40 people. It was generous and exclusive and offered a 40% discount. Once we hit 40 people, it went up to $140 so people felt they were getting a good deal. We knew if we could sell all of these to our closest supporters that we would breeze past our 30% by the end of the day.

We did a lot of research into coming up with the best mix of reward packages to offer. We had a look at what was working for other campaigns and chatted with Pozible about common pledge sizes. Our most popular reward ended up being the Full Supporter, valued at $140, and was chosen by 45 people. For this reward, we gave them a carton of first batch Beach House Ale, a softcover copy of this book, a limited edition Black Hops OG t-shirt, and a Black Hops sticker.

You can even keep some rewards up your sleeve for half-way through the campaign as this will get people excited and back the project again.

In our case the demand for our early bird deal was massive, and we sold our 40 rewards in about one hour. Once we launched to the public, we were past 50%, and within 24 hours, we had hit our target of $10,000.

Press

Five weeks before our campaign launched, we got to work getting the word out. We started reaching out to a list of influencers, press contacts, bloggers, and podcasters that could assist us with publicity.

The key to doing this well was to make sure we'd put together a solid press release with good images and an interesting angle for the story: "Black Hops aiming to become Australia's first brewery to launch via crowdfunding." Leveraging my existing business reputation and the Black Hops story got our foot in the door with press outlets. From there, it was a matter of having a story that created a buzz.

We also tried to be generous and give something back to our early advocates and to the Pozible platform itself, so we backed some other projects on Pozible that resonated with us. It's a good look in the eyes of the platform and and helps raise your own profile.

We also used Thunderclap, which allows you to ask people to pre-schedule a social media update for the date of your launch. For us, it meant 100 people shared the campaign when it launched. We made sure this happened a few hours after we released the early bird deal to ambassadors.

$17,800 earned and major lessons learned

Despite achieving the goal on day one, there were a number of things we could have done better. To be honest, hitting your goal on the first day really isn't as good as it sounds. You want to make the most out of your crowdfunding campaign and it's harder to get people excited once a goal is reached.

Here are some of the things I think we could have done better, which I know would have resulted in us raising even more money.

Understanding crowdfunding goals

The challenge with setting goals for crowdfunding is you don't want to miss your target, but you also don't want to leave money on the table. It's well and good to say you need $10,000 to achieve something, but this is business we are talking about, and for many projects, having $100,000 is much better than having $10,000.

After we passed our 10k goal, we felt a bit awkward rallying the troops to raise even more money. We felt like it was a bit dishonest to say, "Yeah the $10,000 we needed is great, but really, we need a lot more than that."

It's a hard message to communicate to people, but it was the truth. $10,000 would pay for our bottling machine, but it wouldn't come close to covering all of the costs of opening our brewery. Our costs were skyrocketing, our timeframe was blowing out, and we needed every cent we could get. Unfortunately, we struggled to communicate this well, so we didn't raise as much as we could have.

It's critical that you understand your goals and how you are going to manage communications after you hit your target. This also goes back to the first question of why someone should buy from you. If it's just an epic product and you want to sell shitloads of it, then the goal might not be much of a roadblock. But if it's a story-driven exercise where people feel like they are getting behind the idea, this story needs to be carefully managed.

In the end, we raised an amount of money that was good, but wasn't as much as we needed. We had to go back to investors for more money, which is really what we wanted to avoid.

I would have set our goal much higher if we had our time again because raising money after we hit our goal didn't really work. We didn't publicly announce or really speak about any bigger goals for our campaign, but I was hopeful we would raise $30,000 to $50,000, and I think we probably could have if we managed this part of it well. For example, if we had a goal of $30,000 and raised $10,000 on day one, I think we still would have hit the goal and raised at least $30,000. We would have pushed harder, and people would have been more motivated by the larger goal, which wouldn't have been achieved till closer to the end.

Product photos

You can't really sell anything online without epic photos of exactly what people will be getting. We weren't really in a position to have photos of the actual product. We didn't have a brewery yet, and we didn't have packaging for the beers. We did our best with mock ups from designers and nice looking photos of us, but I think for selling the beer, we would have sold a lot more with professional packaging shots.

Photo quality matters. According to online marketer Jeff Bullas, 67% of online shoppers rate the image quality of a product as "very important" when it comes to selecting and purchasing the product. Most people pay more attention to the image than the information about a product.

If we mocked up some epic product shots of what people were actually buying, we would have sold more.

Deliver regular campaign updates

Make sure you're feeding lots of regular campaign updates to your audience. It keeps them engaged and reinforces trust that you're going to be successful reaching your target. It will also deliver confidence that you will be a success once you launch.

As part of the planning strategy, you need to think through how often you will update people and what for. Try to rally existing backers together to further support the project and make sure it feels like a live ongoing thing.

We did a few updates throughout the campaign, but in hindsight, I think we got a bit distracted with other things and probably didn't do as many as we should have.

It's always a bit of a tricky one. I've been on some campaigns that contact you almost every day and you lose trust in the process, but I think we could have sent a few more than we did.

PayPal account freeze issue

A word of warning: PayPal have a common practice of freezing new accounts while they wait for additional business information. The process of providing the information is painful, and they have a lot of silly rules that slow it down (like you can only upload a few MB for files, and once you've used up your space, you can't remove old docs). It's dinosaur age stuff and it's happened to me a number of times, so I should have known it would probably happen with Black Hops.

I didn't think of it at the time, but the impact for us was big with our PayPal payment option being unavailable for a critical week of the campaign.

I'm guessing this happens a bit, so I think Pozible could warn people about this. We could still take credit card payments directly via Pozible while PayPal was down, but having both options normally means more sales.

Stick to your social media schedule

With our campaign, this side of things was very well planned, but day-to-day distractions sometimes got in the way of executing the strategy.

We had planned to update social media every day or two during the campaign, but we failed to keep to this schedule. We should have made it someone's job or used a scheduling tool to make sure we stuck to it. I'm sure if we had kept the social media presence constant throughout the campaign, we would have raised more.

Prepare for timeframe blowouts

As anyone in business would know, timeframe blowouts sometimes can't be avoided. It's part of the risk associated with crowdfunding. Although we were honest about the risks, it would have been nice to have kept our word to our keenest backers in regards to the launch date.

Setting a launch date was always going to be difficult to predict, but in hindsight, we could have built in more of a buffer. If we had hit our launch date early, then great. As they say, better to under-promise and overdeliver.

But hey, I've supported crowdfunding campaigns that ended up being over 18 months late to launch, so I guess we didn't do too badly!

Hopefully, that provides a good insight into how to make a reward-based crowdfunding campaign work.

Equity-based crowdfunding will probably change the landscape quite a bit, so if that is available in your area, consider how that impacts on the likely success of a reward-based campaign, and consider if it's worth looking at for you.

Our second round of financing

Despite our best efforts, we weren't able to bring our project to life within budget. We were delayed, over budget in a number of areas, and we needed more money.

A few weeks out from opening, we had to raise more money through a combination of two founders and one investor. It meant the investor got a bit more equity and we all got a tiny amount less. We would have preferred to avoid it, but we just couldn't get the doors open without it.

Since this book is about building a brewery, not running one, we haven't gone into too much detail about beer finance. Take it from me, finance will be a huge challenge, and the more money you have access to, the better.

CHAPTER 9

PRODUCT

At some point, you need to work out what you are going to sell to people. There are a lot of things you might consider when trying to work this out. For us, we mainly looked at:

1. What beer we wanted to exist
2. What the market wanted
3. What would be a point of difference

Having a decent pilot brewing system is a must, and we came to our core range of beers by using two pilot systems and brewing 20+ different beers before we opened our doors. Some of the brews included the Eggnog Stout, an Aussie Pale Ale, a Dark Belgian, a Funky Dark Belgian, a Black IPA, a Red IPA, four versions of the Beach House Saison, a Scotch Ale made on Govs' stove, a Grapefruit Berlinner Weisse, an Amber Ale, a Smoked Porter, a Coffee Porter, an XPA, a Grapefruit XPA, a Midnight Pale Ale, a Strawberry Saison, a Raspberry Saison, an 11% French Imperial Eggnog Stout, an Oyster Kilpatrick Stout, a Trifle Pale Ale, a Belgian Tripel, a SMASH beer, and probably much more that we can't remember!

Making this many brews really gave us a great idea of what worked and what people liked. We would regularly share the beers with friends and chat about what worked and what didn't. Sometimes, we'd brew it again to refine the recipe, and the beer would become part of our core range.

Pilot system one

When we first met up on Tamborine Mountain, Govs had recently put together his own small HERMS system made from three chopped-down kegs. It replicated the sort of setup you'd have at a full-scale brewery but with a capacity of about 40-litres.

It had one keg for hot water, another as the mash tun that we filled with grain for the brew, and another as the kettle with a small gas burner underneath. It wasn't the sexiest setup, but we brewed most of our pilot brews on this system including the first Eggnog Stout, and other beers, like our ABC Bomb Black IPA and early versions of our Beach House Ale, with excellent results.

Pilot system two

At a chance outing a few months before we opened, Govs was visiting our friends Debz and Moog, avid homebrewers and local craft beer aficionados. Govs was marvelling at their brew-in-a-bag rig with a 100-litre tank made from an old hot water system with an inbuilt electric element and a big pole and pulley system to remove the grain bag. I don't think Moog realised how epic his setup was until Govs got all excited after seeing it. But once he realised how keen Govs was, he offered to build a replica for Black Hops!

This is the pilot system we are currently using, and it's a much simpler way to brew fast batches. It also means we can brew up to 100-litres at a time if we wanted to brew a commercial keg on the setup.

If you are looking to build a brewery, it's a must to have some sort of system for brewing small pilot batches. Braumeister's are a popular choice, and some breweries like Balter on the Gold Coast have a full 500-litre brewery on-site just for pilot brews.

With our pilot system under control, our attention turned to what sort of beer we would make. The first thing we considered was what we wanted to make.

What beer do you want to exist?

Our whole business started because Eddie decided he wanted an Eggnog Stout to be a thing. This tradition has served us well. If you feel like something should exist, there's a good chance someone else will feel the same way. In the startup world, this is called "scratching your own itch."

As well as Eggnog Stout, our other popular beer, Beach House, came to be via the same method. We all loved Saisons and the Saison Dupont was our go-to celebration beer. But it wasn't the sort of beer you'd drink a lot of, and there weren't really many examples of Saisons being treated like a more common sessionable pale ale or lager. Eddie had an idea to change that.

Saisons had great qualities, like their low bitterness, low hop aroma, and a wheaty dry finish. But the funk often associated with a Saison, the yeasty appearance and spicy hops, could be a turn off. This is where Govs made his tweaks, and he came up with a modern twist on a traditional style by including modern Australian and New Zealand hops and adjusting the fermentation temperatures to make a Gold Coast version of a traditional style.

Finding a point of difference

The other thing we look for in our beer is some sort of point of difference. Like in business, it's much easier to grab attention if there is something different about what you are doing.

One example for us is our Saison, Beach House ale. Having a Saison as our main beer instead of a pale ale is unusual and gives us a point of difference. Another is that instead of following the crowd and brewing a standard IPA, we do quarterly seasonal IPAs, a Red, Black, White, and a standard IPA. This makes it a bit different and keeps people coming back to the cellar door.

We decided to brew a 3% Californian Common instead of a mid-strength IPA, and our first beer was a stout in October!

If your strategy is to make better beer than everyone else out there, you need to be 100% confident you can actually pull that off. If your strategy is to be different, the main challenge is to have enough ideas. Of course, making good beer is always crucial, but you have a bit more leeway with your own styles.

What does the market want?

In the end, you have to sell the beer, and you can convince the market to a point to buy your creations, but people also have their own strong opinions. This is the beauty of having so many pilot beers and also a cellar door where you can sell a full range of beers.

You learn what people like, what they don't like, and you can gradually learn what to make more of.

Our Bitter Fun Hoppy Pale Ale is a good example of this. When we started contract brewing, we had a pale ale as part of our core range called The Gold Coast Pale Ale. It was a nice Aussie pale ale, and there was a reasonable demand from customers for it, but it really wasn't all that much different than our normal pale ale.

A month or so before opening, we decided to contract brew one last batch of Gold Coast Pale Ale, so we had beer to sell to pubs to keep them ticking over. The brew went well, but when it came time to kegging the beer, Eddie noticed it was tasting far more bitter than usual.

We got the beer back to HQ, tapped it and tried it, and it was a lot hoppier and more bitter than usual. When Govs went back and looked at the ingredients, he worked out that we actually put in twice as many hops as we wanted to!

We decided we probably shouldn't sell the beer as Gold Coast Pale Ale, but we had it on tap at the brewery while we worked out what to do with it. After a week or two, the beer mellowed out a bit, and most people who tried it, like tradies and mates, seemed to like it. In conversations with venue owners, Eddie found a few venues who wanted a keg even though it was different to our normal pale ale.

When he delivered a sample bottle to Surfers Sandbar, Andrew, the manager, said, "Bit of fun." This was in reference to having something a bit different on tap. When Eddie got back to HQ, he told us the story and we changed the name to Bitter Fun.

We got our designer, Matt, to do up a cool-looking decal for it, and other venues started asking about it. The beer became popular at our cellar door among our visiting mates, and we fell in love with the brand more and more. In the end, we decided to replace our Gold Coast Pale Ale with the Bitter Fun. We refined the recipe a bit, but because of market feedback, our mistake became one of our core range beers!

What works for you?

There is a wide range of approaches taken to choosing beer styles. Some breweries purely brew IPAs and are doing well, while some are brewing crazy beers with chickens in them and also doing well. At the end of the day, do what works, but make sure you can produce a lot of brews quickly and that you can get it into the hands of real customers before making too many decisions.

Pricing considerations

Once you know what you want to make, you'll have to work out how much to sell it for. This was a big challenge for us; the world of beer sales is complicated and navigating the ins and outs wasn't easy.

We are still in our infancy, so we don't feel like we have a full picture of pricing just yet, but we've learned a few lessons, and here are some of our considerations in pricing our beers.

How much it costs to make

Originally, when we were contract brewing on a 50-litre system, it was costing us around $300 Australian Dollars per keg to produce an average core range beer and we were selling them for the same amount. We didn't want to lose money, but we also didn't want to price ourselves out of the market.

Beer is a scale game. There are some expenses you can't avoid, like alcohol excise duty, for example. But there are others that get significantly less at scale, such as ingredients and staff time.

With our brewery setup, we did some rough calculations to figure out about how much it would cost just in materials to make a 50-litre keg of beer. These were a lot of rough guesses, but we figured out it came to about $150 Australian Dollars just for the materials and excise duty.

On top of that, you'd have to consider things like brewery rent, operational costs, staff costs, depreciation of equipment, storage, delivery, own kegs/keg rental, breakage, etc. We estimated the real costs of an average keg to be around $250 with everything considered. Once you add on GST and a profit margin for the business, you are well over $300. That is a lot more than the big brewers sell beer for, even the bigger craft brewers!

For us, we knew our beer had to be interesting enough for bars because it certainly couldn't be the cheapest option.

Excise duty

In most locations, beer is subject to some kind of tax and requires a licence to manufacture it. In Australia, it comes under excise duty, and the amount payable on a keg of beer can be one of the most significant costs in the beer. We will delve into excise duty in more detail in the Approvals chapter, but for costing purposes, you need to understand how much you will have to pay on a keg of beer.

In Australia, the relevant body is the ATO, and the current rates for excise duty are published on their website.

Bar margins

When we first started, we thought we would be dictated by the bar owners when it came to prices. Would they pay $320? Would they pay $350? We worked out pretty quickly that the bars we were targeting didn't care too much about the price. They had their standard margin that they built into the cost of the beer either way. If they paid $240 for the keg, they'd sell the beer for $6 and people would drink a shitload of it. If they paid $400 a keg, they'd sell it for $12 and people would only buy one, although in this instance the beer had better be good!

It became more about pricing the beer at a level that reflected the style of beer and the venue. Some venues could sell plenty of $12 beers and a one-off keg would be fine at $400. Others struggle to move anything much more than the entry-level price. The bar owner might be prepared to pay it, but the last thing you want is your beer to be stuck on tap for six months.

We also found plenty of venues who wanted beer for less than we could make it, and we left those venues for the bigger brewers.

Competing for tap space

Competing against the bigger brewers and even against the more established craft beer brewers can be tough. There are a lot of things they do that make it hard to get your beer on tap at bars. Things like buying taps or paying setup costs to have guaranteed taps at a bar or heavily discounting beers that are bought in bulk. One free for every ten kegs, or even for every three or four kegs, is not uncommon. You can't blame them; it's in their interest to sell more beer to the same customers and keep their overhead down. It's just a challenge that every small brewer faces.

Competing on price is probably not an option, but you can produce a different product and choose the bars that are more likely to rotate their taps.

Ingredients

The availability of ingredients is another big factor to consider in your product choice. Hops, in particular, are hard to come by, and again, the companies want to sell more of their product to the same customers. It's a much less messy way to run a business, so you can't blame them either.

What it means for new breweries is being careful about what hops you use in a beer and being certain that you will be able to get enough. One thing we've done is use a few different hops in our beers so we could chop and change them if we had to. We weren't brewing beers that relied solely on one hop for their flavour. We also tested out lots of brews with hops that were known to offer an alternative to the popular ones.

Once you have more certainty around your brewing schedule, you can start locking in contracts with the hop suppliers.

Finding good suppliers for other special ingredients is also a must. Our Eggnog Stout, for example, has brandy in it. For our first contract brew, we literally bought 13 bottles of brandy from the bottle shop! Once we set up our brewery, we found a local distillery who could supply it to us in 20-litre cubes.

What is right for you?

Getting the product right is an ongoing challenge that will be present for as long as your brewery exists. Keep testing your own ideas, and equally, see how your customers react to your beers. The winners will emerge soon enough, and they might surprise you.

CHAPTER 10

LOCATION

Choosing our location was one of the most enjoyable aspects of opening our brewery. Because we all live on the Gold Coast, we wanted to bring the full craft beer experience to the area. Therefore, we had a good vision of what we wanted. But what you want is one thing, and another is finding something that's realistic and available. Compromise always comes into play.

Here are some of the things we considered before choosing our final location.

Where we wanted to open

First and foremost, we had our own ideas about where we wanted to open. We had some investors interested in getting us to open in Brisbane, but we wanted to be on the Gold Coast. We all lived here and wanted this for the area.

Eddie and Govs loved the industrial area in Currumbin. It was reasonably close to the beach, compared to other industrial areas, and there was plenty of availability. It was also an up-and-coming area with coffee shops and galleries, a little hidden gem in the southern part of the Gold Coast.

I was keen on the Burleigh and Miami area because this is where most of the action is on the Gold Coast. It's where we all live, where all of the bars are, and is a much more established location for coffee shops and event spaces. The challenge for this area was the availability of space, plus it was also a lot more expensive.

I was happy enough to open in Currumbin, and because the other boys were keen and there were places available, we started looking there.

One thing was for sure, opening on the Gold Coast was not negotiable. You have to be proud of where you're located, so it's important to consider what you want as much as anything else.

The market environment

Your business doesn't exist in a vacuum, so of course it's also important to consider what else is going on in your area. In our case, there was only one other brewery on the Gold Coast at the time. It was located in an industrial area a long way from the tourist or local hot spots and was mainly a production brewery.

We felt that for us, a well-located brewery with a big range of one-off creative beers would be a good match for the local market.

There was also an explosion of bars serving craft beer on the Gold Coast, which seemed to be opening on a weekly basis, all looking for local craft beer.

We knew enough about the market to know that Australia was still miles behind other parts of the world such as the United

States in terms of craft beer's share of the broader beer market. We also knew the Gold Coast was a few years behind other parts of Australia. To us, the timing seemed good for us to open a brewery and tasting room on the Gold Coast.

We looked at a few spots in Currumbin and found one factory that looked great. It was a stand-alone building, where we could have the brewery downstairs and offices upstairs. It was pretty rough and would need a lot of work, but the rent was reasonable and the location was good.

We made an offer with the real estate agent, "Brendo," who was very talkative. That was until we got the podcasting recorder out—then not so much!

Proximity to other breweries

As we got closer to planning our opening, we found out that another brewery was opening up nearby. It was being built by an expert team of business and marketing guys who had experience with a similar model from overseas, as well as some of the world's top professional surfers. One of them was local legend and shark-punching royalty, Mick Fanning. On top of that, they had a brewer from Australia's most successful craft brewery, and they were opening three blocks from the building we were looking at in Currumbin.

We thought about this long and hard and went up and down a bit in relation to how we felt about it. There were moments of worry, moments of excitement, and moments of not really caring what other people were doing. The question of whether it made sense for us to open so close to them, came up often. In the end, we decided that it would be a positive for the area to have a few breweries open up and those guys would bring in a whole new market to the area.

We still don't have the answer on how many breweries are too many for an area. Brisbane had a similar situation, with Newstead and Green Beacon opening up one block apart as two of the first new wave of brewpubs in Brisbane. But both were great breweries in a great location and both did well.

Either way, it's good to know what's going on in your area, and having your ear close to the ground in the beer community is a smart move. Planning a brewery takes a long time, so stay on the lookout early for who's doing what as it might impact on your plans.

Proximity to other aligned businesses

How close the location is to other happening spots in your chosen area is another big consideration. We liked Currumbin because there were cool event spaces, galleries, and coffee shops going in. We also liked it further north because there were big event spaces and lots of bars popping up and the majority of the popular restaurants and night spots.

We'd collaborated with a bunch of businesses already on events, beers, and other initiatives so it's great to choose an area with other aligned businesses. Keep this in mind when considering your location, and head out and meet the local businesses. You'll quickly discover how keen the locals are to have a brewery in their backyard.

Proximity to residents

You also have to consider the local residents when planning your space. One of the first places we checked out in Currumbin was just over the fence from people's houses. We were warned by local businesses that they might not make life easy for us once they found out what we were planning.

This is a tricky one, because residents hear the word "brewery" and expect a giant factory polluting the environment or a pub filled with drunk dickheads. A tasting room for a brewery selling $10 craft beers couldn't be further from either of those things, but people's perceptions need to be considered.

In our case, issues relating to drunkenness, pollution, and lack of parking were all raised. The problem is that if you open far away from where anyone is, you will find it very hard to get people to your brewery.

Ease of access for patrons

If you want to run an on-site tap room, then you really want to be in a location that is convenient for people. Ideally, you want to be close to other bars and restaurants, but those areas are often zoned as retail and not suitable for an industrial brewery.

We looked at fringe areas that were close to the action but in semi-industrial areas. We considered transport options, what sort of hours we'd be running, and thought long and hard about who, when, and how people would come.

Being in a great location is a big advantage for a brewery, but be prepared for the reality of potential compromise when it comes to proximity of residents and cost and size considerations.

Cost of space

While we were looking, we encountered a big range of prices, with some landlords and owners open to negotiating on the price and others absolutely not.

In Currumbin, we thought we would have a fair amount of negotiating power. There were a lot of empty warehouses, and some places had been vacant for a long time. Our first offer to the agent, Brendo, however was rejected with no counter offer. We went back and forth a bit, but it was clear he wasn't going to negotiate too much.

Suitability of building

Breweries have a few important requirements when it comes to the building. In our case, we weren't planning on building anything from scratch; we didn't have the budget for that. Instead, we focussed on existing buildings where not much structural re-work would be required.

Some of the issues we needed to consider included: ceiling height (our tallest tank was four metres high), how solid the slab was (tanks are heavy), availability of three-phase power, and suitability of water and wastewater. We also wanted a building that was not going to fall apart.

You are probably going to have to tweak any space to make it work for your requirements, but if you can get away with just knocking down a few walls, that's a big advantage. If you need to add or remove floors or add structural elements, you are talking big dollars.

Availability of space

Availability will ultimately decide your location. A near-perfect location probably exists, but everyone will want it, and waiting around for months or years doesn't make sense. So you compromise and find something between, and that's more or less how it goes.

Our ideal location was actually in Burleigh/Miami, but in the six-month period we were looking, not one suitable place in the area came up. That was until an email came through about a warehouse in the area. It was in the process of being sold and the new owner thought it would make a great fit for a brewery. His name was Justin, so we nicknamed him Biebs (he doesn't know that).

Biebs had recently contacted a local beer blogger about whether he knew of anyone who would be keen. You may remember him from earlier in the story, Darren 250. We'd become mates with Darren, and he let Biebs know that we were planning on opening a brewery on the Gold Coast and were looking for a space.

I called Biebs and arranged to check out the building at 15 Gardenia Grove, Burleigh Heads. I took one look at the location and got very excited. I used to live three streets away and knew it was an exploding hot spot with cafes and restaurants springing up all over the area.

I drove to the building and met Biebs, and we chatted about the space. It was a big, hideous, yellow building with an identical building next door. We couldn't go inside because he didn't own it yet. A few things still had to fall in place for this location to become ours, but I was hooked.

I let Eddie and Govs know that this was our space, and we started negotiating with Biebs. The rent was reasonable, and he was happy for us to paint both buildings black and to knock down the walls to fit our brewing stuff in.

Biebs acquired the building, and in October 2015, we took over the lease and got to work. Our equipment was due to arrive in December, and we had a lot of work to do.

There was also a caretaker's unit upstairs, and I took on the lease for that space for my other businesses. The dream was real. We were in one of the best industrial locations on the Gold Coast, 20 metres from cafes, 100 metres to bars, 300 metres to the beach, with our fledgling brewery downstairs and an office upstairs. Winning!

Landlord

I've heard so many cautionary tales about people having to deal with difficult landlords that it needs to be mentioned here. Biebs has been an absolute legend to us, and it is very difficult to imagine doing what we have if we had to go through a real estate agent or a difficult landlord to get it done.

You'll get vibes from the agent during the negotiation process. For the space in Currumbin, everything was difficult and nothing was negotiable. It was easy with Biebs, and it's been easy ever since. Dealing direct is a great option if you can get it, but either way, dealing with good people will be a huge benefit.

If you get bad vibes from the agent or the landlord during the negotiation phase, you have to think about the potential headaches of operating out of their space full time.

Where we ended up

In the end, we were able to build our brewery in an epic location right in among the best of what the Gold Coast has to offer. We had to say goodbye to Currumbin, but in hindsight, we were happy to be at least a few kilometres away from the nearest brewery—at least for now.

Building preparation

With our equipment due in a few months, we had a lot of work to do to get ready. In this section I've broken down all of the work that needed to be done. This is going to differ from location to location and brewery to brewery, but it should give you some idea of what's involved.

Ceiling and floor space

Our ceiling height was almost exactly four metres at its highest point. The building was made up of three industrial units that had previously housed three separate businesses.

The first unit had the office upstairs and was only three metres high. All up, we had 230 square metres of floorspace and only around 150 square metres of that was suitable for brewing equipment. Originally, we were hoping for at least 300 square metres of suitable space. It was a big compromise, but one we were more than happy to make for this location.

Since we were creating a brewery and tasting room, the decision of where the tasting room would go was made for us. The front would be tasting room, cold room, and bathroom as well as some additional storage where we'd keep grain and packaging. The back two units would be the brewery.

We had the cone on our largest fermenter customised to reduce the overall height of the fermenter slightly down to about four metres. We hoped it would fit, but we weren't 100% sure. We modified the layout of the brewery with our supplier, and Govs managed to squeeze it all in, but it was tight!

Walls

Of course, having three units was no good, so we had to knock down a small opening between the bar/storage area and the brewery area. We were able to do that with the help of our mate Lindon, a local builder.

It was also super important that we removed the walls between Units 2 and 3, which would form the brewery itself. We engaged a local engineer to come check out the wall, even though we'd been told by local builders that it would be fine. There was a huge structural beam above the wall and solid posts on either side with nothing but a tin roof above it. He said he'd draw something up and send us some specs on what we could do.

We waited a few days for his reply, but it never came. A week went past, and we chased him to see what was up. He said he was busy, and we wouldn't be able to knock the wall down. We think he was probably too busy to work on a small job and was just saying that it wasn't possible to make us go away.

We tee'd up another engineer, through a friend, who had a quick look at the wall, scribbled something on a piece of paper, asked for a carton of beer—then left!

We had our approval, and the next week, the wall came down.

Once the walls were down, we painted the ceiling and walls for what felt like weeks. We scrubbed and sugar soaped them first, and eventually the whole inside of the building was painted black.

Floors

The whole space had very solid concrete floors, which we had confirmed by an engineer. The previous business in Unit 2 was Rossco, a mechanic who had a big hoist and a stack of equipment in there. Rossco moved into the identical building next door so we could take the whole space for the brewery.

After the walls were removed, we were able to acid wash and paint the floors. We used heavy-duty industrial paint designed to withstand the rigours of brewery life.

By this time, it was Christmas Eve, 2015, and we had just been notified that our first container would be delivered that day. I was available, so I hung out at the brewery and finalised the painting of the floor and bought a bunch of fans from Bunnings to make sure the floors dried on time.

There was one problem, though. Something went wrong during the paint mixing process and the floors would not dry. When the equipment arrived the next day, we were forced to move the equipment into place on wet floors and ended up having to repaint them at a reasonable expense!

Getting the equipment in

Getting the equipment out of the containers and into the brewery was a lot of fun. Because of the time our equipment turned up, it was in place before a lot of the location work happened (electrical and plumbing). Ideally, plumbing and core electrical work would be done first, but we were a bit behind when our equipment arrived.

Because the equipment is such a big part of the process, I go into this in much more detail in the next chapter.

Council approval

At this point, we started the process of getting approval for our location. I go into this in more detail in the Approvals chapter. The planning around plumbing and some of the other parts happened while working with Council on approval.

Plumbing and trade waste

Plumbing for the brewery was a huge job. We had our mate Jon Kruger (Kruges) from Kruges Plumbing on hand for all of the plumbing work, which was a huge help. Going through the approvals with Council took months, and the on-site work required was significant.

Where possible, we all helped out. One day Eddie and I had the job of cutting up all of the concrete for the drains. As an office worker, working on tools was a lot of fun but the fumes almost caused me to throw up and pass out!

We got there in the end and the space was there for the drains, with no one being seriously harmed in the process.

Here is a quick list of the major jobs that had to happen for the plumbing to be done:

- First, we had to submit a hydraulic plan to the Council for plumbing approval that covered every pipe, tap, drain, hose cock, filter, toilet, hot water system, meter, etc.

- In conjunction with this, we had to apply for a trade waste licence to allow us to discharge to the sewer. Each Council is different, but most will want some form of pretreatment and testing solution to ensure their sewer standards are met. We spent months working with Council, our hydraulic engineer, and trade waste experts to come up with a system to suit our brewery. Councils are typically very risk averse and if it were up to them, we would have spent about $150,000 on the latest filter, settlement, and treating technology. We knew this was overkill, so it was up to us to argue for a simpler solution. After much negotiation, we arrived at a combined 5,000-litre settlement tank and pH correction pump with controlled discharge to the sewer at around nine litres per minute. This extremely low flow rate gave the Council some peace of mind that even if the system were not meeting the sewer standards, it would be so diluted by the time it made it to the treatment plant that it would pose no additional load.

- On top of all of the water filters, pipes, drains, and hoses we were going to need, we also had to conform to the Council's Food Department standards as a prerequisite for our food licence. The food licence is necessary because beer is considered food as it's prepared on-site for human consumption. These standards are very strict around things like hand washing vs. dishwashing sinks, temperature of water, location of toilet facilities, etc. Contact your local Council, and they will explain to you what they require.

- For our plumbing approval, we found this to be quite an unpredictable process. Once the overall plans were approved, our plumber commenced work in stages, and at each stage, we would have a Council inspector sign off on it before starting the next stage. This made sense, at first. Then we realised that it made a huge difference who did the inspecting! Even when the work was 100% done to the plans that had been approved, certain inspectors would find something they wanted changed, which lead to constant re-work and increased labour and supply costs. This was frustrating and quite unnerving; we had no idea whether they would keep finding things to change. After months of deliberation before approving our plans, it became almost infuriating that they could change their minds after the fact. This is a prime example of unbudgeted expenses that you can't predict, which is why sticking to a strict budget for a brewery is a near-impossible task.

Finally, we got our approval, and we could rest—well, for a few hours at least!

Breweries are still relatively new to Gold Coast City Council frameworks and business guidelines, and we quickly realised that we had a big target on our heads. Make sure you engage with your local Council very early to avoid delays. Always be prepared to go into battle for yourself and explore your options. Council will be looking for the solution that poses the least risk, and it's up to you to prove to them that there's a more viable alternative if one exists.

Electrical

The electrical work required for a job like this was also rather epic. We had good old Mushy on call regularly, and if he wasn't available, we had our other mate, Doorbell, on the case.

Here is a rough breakdown of the electrical work that was needed.

The first step was to make sure we had enough power in the building to run all of the appliances. Most of our equipment was designed to run on three-phase power, which chews a lot of amps. Getting more supply is expensive, so we had that checked out early on. We had about 200 amps available, and if everything was turned on at once, we would draw about 180 amps. Phew!

Any respectable electrical contractor will be able to do the work, but it helps to use someone who has experience in an industrial setting. The building we moved into only had basic 10-amp outlets apart from one three-phase outlet that didn't work, which was good, in a way, because we could start from scratch. We had to install new switchboards to house all of the three-phase and 20-amp circuits, then run power cables to the brewhouse and fermentation control panels.

We then had power and control wires installed to each of the pumps, motors, and solenoid switches. Each tank had its own thermometer well that needed to be wired into the control panel to monitor temperature and actuate the solenoid to either cool or heat the vessel. We had a three-phase outlet installed for our mobile CIP pump and grain mill and had power cords and overload protectors connected to each. The two chiller units to run our glycol system were situated outside and needed power and control cables run to both. They also needed to be calibrated to run in unison or independently as needed.

One of the biggest issues was that many of the components did not have earth cables included. We had to spend time and money having these upgraded.

Another issue we had was that when we were close to getting our boiler installed, our electrician strongly recommended rewiring the entire control panel for the boiler. We hadn't planned on this cost, but it was almost 25 years old and many of the relays were outdated and probably at the end of their lives. It was almost a day's work, but we were able to revitalise and optimise the controls and also have a brand new electrical diagram drawn up to assist with any future faults.

We also had to plan where we wanted outlets and lights, and we needed power for various other pieces of equipment around the cellar door like our hot water system, cold room, alarm system, etc.

Security

Upgrading security was also an important consideration. We didn't want to get broken into, and it made it easier to get licences and more favourable insurance premiums.

We added security cameras, an alarm system, deadbolts on the doors and the roller doors, padlocks on everything, upgraded lighting, and even replaced the front door with a sturdier one. We have a company that monitors the alarm who also put signs around the building. We have strict processes for ensuring cash isn't kept on the premises, along with a number of other security measures.

Ventilation

For our requirements, we installed high and low ventilation in the brewhouse to improve airflow and regulate temperature. We also added a flue kit to the kettle to assist with boil-off and to reduce odours.

For gas boiler compliance, high and low ventilation is required so gas can escape if you have a leak and not fill the room with gas when locked up. It also helps to aspirate the room when the burner is on. We were able to comply with this due to our whirly-birds up high and our drainage, which is 50/50 under the roller door, meaning there is low air flow available under our roller doors.

Cold room

We opted to rent a cold room because we didn't have the funds to buy one. Luckily, we were able to find one the perfect size for our area, and we could customise it a bit to make it work. We ran with a direct pour setup so kegs in the cold room pour directly through taps out the side of the cold room to the bar.

We mounted some old, silky oak doors to the cold room and had our designer draw our new logo on it. Eddie's dad, Martin, made up a menu board for us that sits on the wall off the cold room. The direct pour system is efficient and works well, although the cold room noise was a bit of a compromise. We added some sound deadener above it to reduce the impact a little bit.

Bar

My friend Fiona gave us some design advice for the tasting room area. None of us had much experience with this sort of thing, and we also didn't have a budget for it. With some ideas from Fiona, and the skills of Martin, we managed to cobble a solution together: a second-hand sink, a stainless bench sourced online, a big wooden bar sourced through Eddie's uncle Clive, and corrugated iron "borrowed" from out the back of Rossco's Mechanical Repairs. The bar was taking shape.

We also hired equipment from Bunnings for grinding and polishing the bar floor, which turned out great. We had a local graffiti artist design and spray paint one of the walls, and Martin built a nice bathroom for guests and a gate through to the main storage area.

Eddie sourced the lights, which were installed by Mushy, and we were good to go.

The cellar door area is small due to our restrictions with the Council, but it's a nice little space to host small groups, serve people a beer, and sell takeaways.

Back area

We also had an area out the back that needed a bit of work. This is where we placed the gas bottles and the chillers for the glycol. We also filled in the door for security because we didn't really need it, and we gated off the back area.

Next to the gate, we installed a basketball ring for when we had a bit of down time.

Lab and brewery bathroom

We had very little funds for anything flashy, but we were able to get Martin to put together a basin, toilet, and lab area at the back of the brewery. Our lab is only about one square-metre, but with some shelving, it gives us enough room for lab equipment.

Steam boiler

Equipment and location wise we were just about ready. Govs ran a brewery test with water, and it all looked good. All we needed to do now was set up the steam boiler to give us the steam to heat up the water.

It had all gone reasonably smoothly up until now. It was around April 2016, and we were a few months behind a very ambitious schedule, but for the most part, we felt we'd done well.

Unfortunately, it was all about to go to shit. But let's save that story for the Fuckups chapter.

CHAPTER 11

EQUIPMENT

To meet our budget requirements, we decided early on to source our equipment from China. This ended up being the best decision we made, but it was also the part of the process we spent the most amount of time on.

What you need to know about doing business in China

China has a bit of a bad reputation in the brewing industry. When we started out, most people were buying equipment from Europe or the U.S. from the well-known brewery suppliers. People's experience with China was that the gear was bad quality and not worth the hassle. We figured out early on that most of the expensive stuff was being made in China anyway, and we were up for the challenge of figuring out how to make it work. Plus, we simply couldn't afford any other option.

The Chinese manufacturers tend to operate on the principle that the lowest price can get them the sale, thus compromising on quality. They also don't have much of a craft beer scene, and some manufacturers were making equipment without knowing much about how it was to be used.

The equipment supplier we chose, Tiantai in Jinan, had been on a growth curve of improving quality over the years. It happened because, as they sold more and more overseas, customers became better at explaining exactly what they expected.

Their pump and brewing equipment suppliers improved, welds were getting better, and the type of stainless steel improved. We knew this because we'd chatted with some of their customers leading up to the purchase.

We went through a rigorous six-month process of speaking with the relevant people, analysing the business, and talking with other brewers about what to look for. In short, we did our research!

We were very impressed with our choice when we first visited their factory and saw the quality on display. More about our China trip a bit later.

Choosing a supplier

This is by no means a definitive list for choosing a brewery supplier; there are many variables to consider. As we dug into it, we found that there were generally three options for sourcing a supplier in China:

1. Find a company in China that is managed by Westerners. We discovered a few promising options. They were significantly more expensive than going direct, but cheaper than buying outside of China.

2. Find a local consultant who works with a preferred supplier in China. You deal with the local person, and they deal with a factory with whom they are used to dealing.

3. Go direct to the factory.

Option three is a very high-risk option. You have to be prepared to go to China and do a lot of research on your provider. Even then, you probably have to expect some curveballs. However, it will be a lot cheaper. In our case, we spent less than half of what others spent to get up and running. We figured some of the money we saved would be eaten up in fixing issues once the equipment arrived in Australia, but we were prepared to take the risk because we literally couldn't afford any other option.

What to look out for

When buying brewing equipment in China there are a few things you'll want to look for in terms of quality. You really need to know what you are doing, but in our case here were some of the things we kept an eye out for:

1. The quality of welding won't be perfect and will often be inconsistent. For example, some welds will look perfect, others a little bit messy. Internal welds on tanks are the most critical, and there is a big difference between an imperfect weld on the exterior and a bad weld on the interior.

2. The quality of the stainless steel is important. We asked for certificates of quality and details on the thickness of the stainless as well as photos at every step of the process. When we visited the factory, we checked out the raw sheets of stainless and observed the whole process from raw material to final brewery.

3. The items that are brought into the factory from external suppliers can be problematic. You really need to know your suppliers and the quality of equipment they supply. This could mean sourcing pumps and other items elsewhere or making sure you know exactly what you are getting.

4. Some items, such as a steam boiler, you are probably better off buying locally.

5. Sometimes a manual item is better. For example, we were a bit nervous about the automatic keg washer, so we went for a manual one. It's best to avoid unnecessary complication because replacing items once you are up and running isn't going to be cheap or easy.

What happens in China goes to print

Out of all of the advice we got, one message kept coming up: Be sure to go and inspect your equipment. So we did.

Now, I'd love this chapter to be actionable and practical, but it would be negligent of me not to detail the events of our first (and possibly last) China trip.

On the first of October, we left the Gold Coast, headed up to Brisbane airport, necked a few quick Newstead IPAs at the departure lounge at 9:00 a.m. and jumped on a 9-hour flight destined for Guangzhou. Once on the plane, we soon learnt that the Chinese drink their beer at room temperature. No problem for us, the beer was free, and according to the wrap on the can, it was "excellent quality." Because we were excited about our Chinese adventure, we all agreed, "This isn't too bad!"

The word for beer in Chinese is "píjiǔ."

We only learned four words in China: píjiǔ, gānbēi (cheers), xièxiè (thank you, pronounced "shit yeah" in Aussie), and Jana. They all came in handy.

Day one - China meet Black Hops

Qingdao to Jinan

Guangzhou is apparently the second largest airport in China, and it felt every bit of it. We caught buses and golf buggies, crossed multiple highways, and travelled fuck knows how many kilometres just to connect to another flight to Qingdao in the northeast of China. The queues at every point were hectic and hot, but in the end, our three-hour layover turned into 30 minutes at the gate.

Qingdao, a three-hour flight from Guangzhou, was our final stop for that day. Qingdao is the port where our equipment would be sent out from, but not our ultimate destination. It was after midnight when we landed and we had a hotel booked for that night before heading to Jinan by train the next day.

Qingdao, in China's eastern Shandong province, is a port city of skyscrapers, parks, and beaches bordering the Yellow Sea. If that sounds familiar, it's because I stole it from Wikipedia. All we knew was that it was the only way to get to Jinan where our equipment supplier, Tiantai, was.

Apparently, Qingdao is known for its beer. It was once occupied by the Germans who opened a brewery in 1903, and the Qingdao International Beer Festival is kind of a big deal. The brewery (now called Tsingtao, producing the national beer of the same name), still operates and has a beer museum on site.

We were staying at the Sheraton and had pre-arranged a taxi through the hotel, which made it easy, and before long we were on wi-fi on our phones in bed.

We were about to go to sleep when Govs excitedly announced, "Looks like Qingdao has a craft brewery!" Going to the beer museum was on the agenda, but a craft brewery was always going to take priority.

He'd found a local brewery on Google (which we could access thanks to our pre-arranged VPN service), and we all agreed to suss it out first thing in the morning. We had a whole day to make the train, so we had time to check out the local sights.

At 8:00 a.m., we headed out in search of the Strong Ale Works Brewery. After a failed attempt to book an Uber, we had the concierge book us a cab to an unknown location by the sea. We pulled up at the address we found on TripAdvisor, which looked more like some rich guy's house than a brewery. We ignored the gigantic German Shepherd dogs and strolled in after a few ales. Eddie tried to have a conversation with them, which went nowhere because, as we were very quickly learning, no one speaks English in China.

I Googled around some more and found a number online to give a call. The boys watched on, expecting me to be having another go-nowhere conversation with a Chinese dude who didn't understand a word of mine. But instead, I got John, an American, who was the brewery owner, and he said he'd be there in 30 minutes.

We met him behind the back of the houses in an epic-looking little brewery with an adjoining art gallery. It was the kind of setup you'd find in Melbourne full of hipsters except this was China, and we were the only bearded people in sight!

John had a 500-litre brewery that came from Tiantai. At this point, just knowing that this company was actually real was a relief for us. We found them on Alibaba, after all, and we'd all had the nightmare of rocking up to China to find out there was no such company.

John was also making some solid beer, which was great to see, and he told us to make ourselves comfortable.*

*Tip for international readers, don't ever tell Aussies to make themselves comfortable.

We settled in for the day, watched John get filmed for the local TV station, and even got in the footage ourselves. Getting on TV in China wasn't high on our list of priorities, but it was a nice bonus.

John then agreed to go out for lunch, so we shouted him lunch at a local restaurant. As we walked in, we looked at all of the various seafood options lying on the floor, unrefrigerated, and ordered pretty much every one of them.

We ate garfish, noodles, beans, normal fish, some other non-normal looking fish, eel, and a massive bowl of chicken hearts. The guilt kicked in when we realized that a whole chicken had to die for every heart in the hundreds of hearts in this bowl, and even harder when we left half a bowl uneaten!

They were also serving "excellent quality" beer in tallies, and it wasn't long before the shitfacededness took over the guilt.

It was nearing afternoon, and we had to catch a train by 6:00 p.m. and had absolutely no idea where we were or where we needed to get to.

Luckily, we had John, and apparently, he hadn't been drinking as much as us. He drove us to some lady in a bunk bed to buy tickets (we didn't ask any questions), and onto the train station. We got there with 30 minutes to spare, which meant we could buy beer from the takeaway store and drink it at the station. No one seemed to mind us drinking in public, but the Dark Ale was so revolting that there was no chance of it becoming a mainstream problem.

If you ever find yourself in Qingdao, we highly recommend finding yourself a John. Strong Ale Works is located inside the 138 Art Warehouse on the corner of Hailong Road and Hongkong Road (Xianggang Road). I hope you have more luck finding it than we did.

First class on the Jinan Tea Express

We upgraded to first class tickets (seats with recliners and leg-room) as it was a 1,000-km ride. Since this was a train that travels 300 km/h, it was a quick trip at around three hours.

After the train took off, we quickly left our first class cabin and looked for greener pastures (i.e., a cabin that sold beer). We arrived at what looked a lot like the drinks cabin. There were three girls working at the counter, and we asked them if we could sit down and drink píjiǔ. They didn't have a clue what we were saying, and visa versa, so we all agreed with body language that we should sit down.

They said a few things, we pointed to beer, and eventually we were greeted with more warm Tsingtao, much to our delight.

As we played cards and drank beer, the waitress continued to bring different versions of pretty rank-tasting tea out. The girls behind the counter giggled, and we nodded our heads, kept drinking the warm beer and didn't touch the tea.

My experience in Asia came in handy here. I'd travelled to Vietnam before, and I reassured the boys that it's custom in Asia to give people free tea water on arrival.

About 2.5 hours flew by, and all of a sudden the counter girls were signalling to us that this was our stop. We went up to pay what we thought would be about $30 and were greeted with a $300 USD bill.

Whatever the fuck they put in that tea, it was expensive, or we just got majorly touched. Either way, we had a few minutes to drop it like it was hot and get out of there. Problem was, we had no cash.

Again, my experience travelling in Asia came in handy. I'd ensured the guys that Asia was cheap and everywhere had eftpos. No need to carry a lot of local cash.

Unfortunately, as we would discover, this was not the case in China.

We scraped together whatever Chinese Yuan we had, but it was nowhere near enough.

I'd started trying my cards one by one on their eftpos machine. Meanwhile, the train was slowing as we were coming into Jinan, and we were about half a train away from our bags, which were back in "first class". We agreed that Eddie and Govs would sprint back to the cabin, get our bags, and rush back to me.

I kept trying my cards, a Black Hops Visa Debit card, a U.S. Business Amex Card, an Australian Visa Credit Card, an Australian

Business ANZ Debit card, my personal ANZ Debit Card—every one failed.

I started to worry for real, and the girls behind the counter were no longer giggling. The train slowed to a near stop, and the one girl who spoke a few words said something about the next stop being Beijing.

The train stopped, the doors opened, and Eddie and Govs came rushing into the cabin with our bags.

She then suggested that she message us on WeChat. I gave her my WeChat code, and we all looked at each other and jumped off the train as the doors were closing.

Its 400 km to Beijing, and we weren't keen at all to visit the Chinese capital at that point.

I sent a few messages on WeChat ensuring the train lady that we'd pay back the $300 USD.

Relieved, we made it off the train and walked up to the car park to be greeted by Ray and Jana from Tinantai. Ray was the GM, so we knew we had to behave ourselves.

Jana was the person we had been dealing with for the last 10 months. She was a sweet little Chinese woman who was put through her paces when Black Hops came to town. First on the agenda was figuring out how to pay back the train company. Jana said it was no problem and got in contact with the train girl on WeChat and made an arrangement for us to pay back the money.

Jana and Ray took us to a huge Chinese restaurant with multiple levels and a lot of cigarette smoke. Again, we ordered pretty much everything on the menu, beer (this time the Tsingtao Wheat Beer) and food. We drank even more warm beer and stayed for hours eating. Deep fried chicken, three types of dim sums, beans, broccoli, and, of course, the favorite of the night, cicada enchiladas. The favourite because (a) it was a bug, and (b) it rhymed, and after 16 hours of drinking warm beer, everything is entertaining. Little did I know, the entertainment would go up to a whole new level.

We finished up and headed back to our new hotel. I, for one, was stoked to see a bed, and we all laid in our beds, looking forward to our visit to the Tiantai factory the next day.

I drifted off to sleep, and so did Eddie and Govs. Or so I thought.

We have a little bit of a situation

"Oi, oi, Dan!" I forced one eye open to see Eddie nudging me.

Our first day in China had been a big one. I was happily sleeping, not really ready for it to get bigger.

It was 11:45 p.m., and I was in the sweet spot between pissed and hungover, still feeling like you would if you ate half of China. I was smart enough to call it a night after the feast, but apparently Eddie and Govs kicked on. As I drifted off to sleep, they figured they'd check out the hotel bar.

I suspected I was about to hear the outcome of that decision.

Eddie sat at the end of my bed looking down at me, much like a concerned father might be if he was about to have a heart-to-heart with his son. "We have a little bit of a situation," he explained.

I tend to worry a bit too much, and despite my state, I started putting two and two together. Eddie was there but Govs wasn't. Eddie was concerned. As I heard him out, I thought there's a reasonable chance that Govs was dead.

The good news was, he wasn't. At least not yet.

When I crashed out, the boys had wandered into the karaoke bar next door and ordered a few beers (warm, I assume). They were brought watermelon as Govs did his best Robbie Williams impersonation on the karaoke. Eddie grew more and more nervous. First, extra beers, then the watermelon, then a group of girls and some dice. He started thinking that maybe they shouldn't spend too much more time at the karaoke venue, or KTV as it said on the sign. Govs had moved onto Dr Dre.

"So, long story short," he explained. "We got the fuck out of there and went to pay the bill, which was $1,400 Chinese Yuan (about $300 Australian dollars)! They speak no English, so we couldn't argue it. The problem is that none of our cards work, and now we have pimps chasing us."

This seemed familiar, so again I figured I could help by trying every card known to mankind as a method of payment. I figured Eddie thought the same or he wouldn't have been waking me.

I went down to help deal with what has since become known as "the little situation." Again, I tried every card in my wallet, both on their eftpos machine and on the ATM at the hotel, and nothing worked.

There were quite a few characters in this circus. There was the boss, the "waitresses" who were waiting to get paid, the more vocal one who was dressed a bit nicer and seemed to have some relationship with the boss, and the pimp. The pimp was a fat Chinese guy dressed like 50 Cent in a basketball jersey, shorts, and big chains. He was the one doing the negotiating.

Of course, they couldn't speak English, so the pimp had an English translation app on his phone, trying to translate everything we were saying.

It was quite the scene. I wasn't sure whether to piss myself laughing or shit myself scared. In the end, the best we could do was negotiate for us to leave a phone and meet back in the morning to pay the debt. We figured that this was a good outcome, and while it was probably unlikely that we would be chopped up into small pieces by the pimp, it was a possibility.

Day two - Tiantai factory visit

The pimp transfer

The next day, we met Jana for the factory tour, and she helped us resolve the little situation. She drove us to the bank where our cards worked, and we returned to the foyer where we'd agreed to meet the pimp. Jana and I waited anxiously, and after a few minutes, he emerged out of a van wearing the exact same gangsta clothes from the night before.

Eddie and Govs waited in the car while Jana and I completed the transfer. I paid him the cash, and he even brought the receipt, which I thought was considerate given the nature of the transaction. I asked for it (for tax purposes), but he shook his head and shuffled off.

When Jana saw the bill, she giggled and asked inquisitively, "How long did you sing for?!"

Lesson learned. If you want to do karaoke, do it on the street (more on that later). If you go into a bar with a big red KTV sign out front, expect a little more than karaoke and some seriously expensive watermelon.

Tiantai factory visit

After "the little situation," we pressed on with our plans for the day.

The factory was about 40 minutes outside of downtown Jinan, and Ray and Jana were keen to show it to us.

We were given lots of warnings about doing business in China. Things they might say, things they might do, etc. Examples included, if they say "don't worry," you probably should worry. Or if they say "no, don't go into that room," go into that room!

We were also told countless times that they can make stuff really well, but they need to be given lots of guidance as they don't know how to use the things they are making. There is no doubting that the Chinese make all of the best stuff we take for granted and use every day. Govs spent about 10 months, with thousands of emails back and forth to the company, fine-tuning the brewery layout and our equipment needs. We spoke to many people, and we got lots of quotes, so we did do our homework.

One of the coolest things that happened when we arrived at the factory was when Jana asked if we wanted a beer. We said yes, assuming it would be another warm Tsingtao plucked from the kitchen bench. She opened a door with the words "Craft Brewing Room" on it and revealed a fully functioning brewery in the office! The brewers poured us a jug straight from the fermenter. This was great because we were told they know how to make equipment but don't know how to use it. That theory was wrong.

We then began a full tour of their factory. They had 5,000 square metres of floor space, and there were fermenters and brewhouses in all stages of their builds, as far as the eye could see. We were shown our fermenters and kettle and mash tun and lauter tun; it was all very exciting. They weren't as far into the production as we were hoping, which was a bit of a bummer as we were hoping to see it at about 90% complete. Unfortunately, it was probably closer to 70%. A one-week holiday the week before we visited was apparently a bit of a set back as they hadn't factored that in. However, we got to inspect everything under the shiny stainless steel outer, and it all looked amazing. We saw our mill, our pumps, our keg washer, and our glycol tanks—everything looked great.

Whilst we didn't get to see the finished product of our own order, they had several that were complete, so we were able to look over them very carefully. We were blown away by the quality. The factory itself was also extremely tidy, nothing was off limits as the factory was just one big open plan space. Everything we saw reassured us that we had made the right decision.

We spent a few hours wandering around and took hundreds of photos and a bunch of videos. We then went back to the boardroom and discussed a few things, mainly around the timing for completion.

That was that; we had seen what we had travelled so far to see. Jana and Ray took us to lunch back in downtown Jinan to a German-themed brewpub, serving up a pretty tasty hef. They drove us around town after that, pointing out the different tourist attractions.

They then left us at the Manoa Springs to "sightsee" and walk around and experience Jinan. We looked at the water for about three minutes and then headed straight to a bar with a Chimay umbrella out the front.

We were stoked to find a Belgian beer cafe overlooking the Springs serving up Chimay, Lindemans, and Delirium on tap! Not only that, we were right in the middle of two-for-one happy hour. We ordered a few beers and something wasn't 100% right. The beers tasted very average, and the owners wouldn't let us take photos of the taps. After a few beers, the penny dropped. No doubt about it, the tap beer was counterfeit. Luckily, they had about 50 incredible Belgian beers in bottles, so we made the switch.

Our sightseeing turned into spending the whole afternoon at this place. We ordered 30 beers in total between the three of us, almost all of them over 8%. Some of them included Tripel Karmeliet, Rochefort 10, Westmalle Dubbel and Delirium Tremens, Red, and Nocturnum. We had successfully spent $300 on beer in China, and for the first time, on purpose!

On the way out, we stumbled across some very average street karaoke and Govs couldn't help but try to redeem himself from the KTV ordeal. He dropped "Nuthin' but a 'G' Thang," I followed it up with "Bitches Ain't Shit," and China learnt what real karaoke was all about. The next night, the guy running the karaoke texted me asking us to come back for another performance. By that time, we were headed back to the airport, it was one night and one night only.

In the morning of our final day, I had an early flight to Bangkok for a conference. Jana picked me up and took me to the airport and returned to Govs and Eddie for a tour of the Tiantai office. It was cool to get a glimpse inside the company. It was very much like an Australian office, with motivational posters, KPIs, and team goals on whiteboards, cubicles, and computers. It felt like we were dealing with a good company and gave us more peace of mind.

The day before at the Tiantai factory, we had seen a small four-head manual bottling line that took our fancy. Govs asked Jana for some info on it, and she returned with a brochure and some pricing. The boys confirmed there was enough room in our container to squeeze it in, and they agreed to buy it. We had always planned to get one, but it was going to come later. It was love at first sight, and once we saw it, we had to have it.

Jana took Eddie and Govs out for a final lunch to a dumpling bar a few streets away, where the food was amazing. They then headed back to the factory for a final quick look around and a game of pool and table tennis before heading off to the airport to fly home.

It was an epic trip. Jana and Ray had been amazing hosts, and we had a lot of fun. The equipment looked amazing, and the company was legit. We went home relieved and excited.

Our setup

For this section, I asked Govs to chip in with all of the details on what we ended up going with. If you are into the technical stuff, this is for you. If not, feel free to skip to the next section.

As a bit of a bonus, the system we ended up getting was quite a bit oversized. It's normal for tanks to be a bit oversized, but ours were surprisingly big. Our 20-HL (hectolitre) tanks were more like 25-HL and our 40-HL fermenter was more like 50-HL.

Here is a list of the major pieces of equipment in the steam-powered brewery we ordered:

- 20-HL three-vessel brewhouse
- Hot/cold liquor (HLT)
- Mash tun (decoction capable)
- Lauter tun and kettle/whirpool
- one x 40-HL, three x 20-HL and one x 10-HL conical fermenters (FVs)
- one x 40-HL bright beer tank (BBT)
- 2 x 7hp glycol chillers
- one x PDL bag filter
- one x manual double-station keg washer
- one x mobile pump for CIP and transfer
- 800 kg/h Malt Crusher mill
- 4-head counter-pressure bottle filler
- 20-m^2 heat exchanger
- Two control boards, one for the brew house and one for fermentation

We first contacted Tiantai in late 2014 (amongst many other suppliers) and spent the next six months making changes to the proposed system. Some of these decisions were made by Govs based on his experience and preference, some were made after speaking to their past customers. One customer, in particular, was Luke from Coda Brewing who went into a lot of detail about changes for us to consider.

The motive for these changes was to first, improve the design of the equipment and second, to remove some of the expensive automated processes that could be difficult to repair/replace if they failed. Here are some of the changes and reasons for each:

1. We added a side port to the kettle in addition to the bottom center drain. They now have two ports at the bottom of the kettle/whirlpool tun. One is in the center for drainage, the other is on the side of the kettle for removing the wort.

2. We asked them to confirm, with images, the polishing of all welds. They have strictly improved the polishing of all welds.

3. We confirmed that they had sight glasses on the BBT. This is standard in their equipment now.

4. We confirmed that they have added Pressure Release Valves (PRVs) to BBTs. They confirmed they have removed the solenoid relief valve from tanks and all pressure gauges have oil and are good quality with PSI/MPA display.

5. We confirmed the presence of adjustable legs on all vessels. They improved the quality of the pad as some of the older ones rusted (after speaking with other customers).

6. We made sure that they provided an upgraded carbonation stone for the BBT to be easier to clean in place. This is now standard.

7. We had them add a sight glass to the kettle. It is standard, now, on both the kettle and HLT to have a sight glass.

8. We specifically requested they increase the size of the heat exchanger from 12 m^2 to 20 m^2 for more efficient chilling of the wort. It's big for what we need, but bigger is better!

9. We confirmed that they had increased the size of the stainless from 2 mm to 3 mm. This is now standard with all interior shells at 3 mm (11 gauge) and exterior shells at 2 mm (14 gauge).

10. We sourced our boiler locally in Australia since Chinese boilers can be difficult to get approved, but that's another story for later in this book!

11. We added rotating racking arms to the FVs instead of stand pipes. This is now standard. The racking arm in the cone is rotating.

12. We added steam to the mash tun for decoction mashing.

13. We added a square manway to the lauter tun instead of a round one. A square manway for spent grain out is now standard.

14. We had them use a dome bottom, not conical bottom, on the BBT for more even carbonation.

15. We requested that the HLT have a fin or offset pipe to prevent whirlpooling.

16. We confirmed that the electrical components were to our local requirements. For Australia, we are using parts with a UL or a CUL certificate, mostly Siemens or LG brand.

There were also a few things we changed after the visit, which are now standard on their systems:

1. We got an extra pump inline from the HLT to the manifold for fly sparging.

2. We now have a sight glass on the HLT.

3. We upgraded the v-wire false bottom to a laser cutting type.

4. We added larger piping on the bottom of the FVs to prevent clogging from trub.

5. We added two arms on the FVs: one CIP and one blow off.

6. We added an extra 1.5-inch Tri-clover on the BBT and FVs for sample port/recirculating finings/hops.

7. All legs on the FVs and BBT had braces added.

8. We instructed that the bottom of the FVs and BBT be tri-clamped not welded.

There were also things we let them know about after we got our equipment. One example was not having earth cables on the electrical components. We let them know that this is a requirement to meet Australian safety standards, and they now include them as standard for Australian orders.

Lab setup

Having a quality control lab is vital to ensuring the quality and consistency of your beer; however, it can be very expensive to set up. We did a lot of research on innovative ways to perform those important tests without blowing the budget. Here is a quick rundown:

- Gravity and pH - We bought locally-made and ATO-calibrated hydrometers and an upmarket handheld pH meter.
- Sterilisation - Instead of an expensive autoclave to sterilise our parts and yeast-handling utensils, we bought a commercial pressure cooker that is capable of the required pressure and temperatures to effectively sterilise these tools.
- Quality Control - To grow our yeast plates and test for bacterial growth, we bought a baby cloth warmer on eBay, which makes for a perfect incubator.
- Cell Counts - Finding an inexpensive secondhand microscope and hemocytometer is quite easy and becomes an invaluable tool for doing yeast cell counts and viability tests.
- CIP Titration - Talk to your chemical supply company, and ask if they can supply you with the necessary tools and reagents to be able to test the titration levels of your cleaning chemicals. This is to ensure you are effectively cleaning and sanitising your equipment.

If you want to see a complete list of our equipment with prices, head to blackhops.com.au/book and you can get it for free. There are also some great tips available at brewingscience.com.

Organising delivery

It was getting to the point where we needed to sort out how our kit would get from the port in China to Brisbane, and then from Brisbane to the Gold Coast. This was all very new to us, so naturally, we spoke to a number of people about it before deciding on someone to help us.

One of the pieces of advice we were given was to not let the Chinese provider handle it as you can end up paying twice for certain charges. We got a bunch of quotes from freight forwarding companies; some were randomly selected, while others were based off someone else having used them. In the end, we went with Laurie at CargoClear. CargoClear are based in Brisbane and were who Wade at Four Hearts had used.

I'm pretty sure that we still don't really understand the range of quotes we were given because the taxes and charges that appear on them are mind boggling. The price difference between the various quotes on paper was up to $15,000. In the end, however, the quotes seemed to balance out, and we ended up paying more than we were quoted.

One of the things that will potentially cost money was a classification on the tariffs of what we were importing. The number one thing you need to know is that in Australia, brewing equipment is duty free. Your freight forwarder will not necessarily make this known because it's their job to ask questions and not make suggestions. We had a bit of confusion around the classification involving the controllers, and in turn, did not import our gear as brewing equipment. Unfortunately, we ended up paying over $7,000 in duty by mistake. We discovered this error the day before our equipment arrived and had the option to dispute. The problem was, the potential to delay our delivery (at a cost of over $1,000 per day) was real, and could quite easily have totalled more than our refund. Luckily we were able to claim this after the containers had been delivered and it was refunded in full.

Basically, the job of the freight forwarder is to work with the manufacturer to coordinate getting the order onto the ship, through Customs at the other end, and delivered to your door. There are a number of costs involved; we budgeted $24,000 based on some advice we were given very early on to allow for around $6,000 per container, which was fairly accurate. However, the taxes on top of that were never mentioned. It ended up costing $34,000 delivered to our door, which was a hell of a lot more than we were expecting.

Fumigation is another thing to look into. If you are bringing wood into the country (for example, timber pallets), it needs a fumigation certificate, otherwise quarantine will hold it and charge you for doing it locally. Bring this up with the supplier so it doesn't become a problem.

Another issue we ran into was that when our equipment arrived at the port in Brisbane, the Chinese freight forwarder said they hadn't been paid by Tiantai and told CargoClear not to release it to us. Getting equipment stuck at the port can mean thousands of dollars in storage fees.

Govs and Eddie chased Tiantai via message and phone and within an hour or so Tiantai were able to contact the provider and confirm it was paid. That was a bit of a heart-stopping moment, but luckily Tiantai were able to help us out relatively quickly.

We still aren't exactly sure how the costings worked as we found the process very confusing. The best thing we can suggest is to have a trusted partner to work with and budget it at the higher end because it can get expensive quickly.

Equipment received

When we inspected our equipment in China, it was about 70% built, so we were able to get a good idea of the quality. We were also able to see a number of completed orders prior to them being sent out. The trip was well worthwhile and very comforting, but still, we were all nervously awaiting the delivery of our finished brewery.

The communication leading up to the delivery was very good with Tiantai. Up until our trip, emails were very forthcoming, however pictures were few and far between. This wasn't really a bother, but pictures are pretty damn cool to see. One of the things we requested on the factory visit was weekly picture updates.

Containers arrived

All of the hard work of the last nine months had finally paid off, and our first 40-foot container arrived at 7:00 a.m. on Christmas Eve. We could not have been more excited to finally have our gear on location.

As I mentioned before, the floor prep had started this same day, so we didn't start to unload the container until the next day, but we did manage to pose for some selfies with the shiny stainless bling. Best Christmas present ever!

The deal with the containers and port storage is you get 10 days free at port. For first-time importers, you are almost guaranteed to be held and X-rayed at Customs, which we were, so that eats into your 10 days. By the time our four containers got through, we had five days remaining before we had to start paying $250 per container per day. Our other challenge was that due to our site, we had to stagger the delivery because we could only fit one container at a time. We wanted to avoid any additional charges, so we had to learn how to unload a brewery fast and with minimal gear.

Unloading

With the site prepared as best we could, we cracked open the first container on Saturday December 26, 2015 to assess what needed to be done.

After a trip to Bunnings to buy the most badass straps, shackles, and ratchets we could find, we were good to go.

We attached the strap to our 1,000-litre fermenter and our forklift and started to drag it out. We still have no idea how they got this tank into the container, as it was not only our smallest tank, it was also the one that took the most time to get out. They had it standing up, but the height of the tank was taller than the opening of the container, so we had to angle it enough to pull out. It took us five hours. The day was over, and we had one tank out.

Sunday was better. We emptied the majority of the first container, and we were getting the hang of it. We finished the first container

Monday morning and were ready for the second container to arrive on Tuesday.

We are very lucky to have such a supportive community of friends who offered their time to help us to unload the equipment. It was awesome to have help from mates during this, and we could not have done it without them. A lot of free beer was earnt that day!

By the fourth container, we were pretty awesome at unloading tanks. Sideways, upright it, didn't really matter, we had it sussed. The final tank we pulled out was our 40-hectolitre fermenter. We had this built a little shorter and a little stouter than usual to allow for our four-metre-high roof. This was nerve-racking because, until it was standing upright, we had no idea if it was going to fit. We had our mates Byron and Dick come in and assist with taking off the roof so we could get the forklift mast up and above the ceiling height. From there we could lift it from above and slowly stand it up—and it fit. Just!

After a lot of moving around, everything was in the building and in its rightful place.

Build quality and the piecing together

With all of the brewing gear safely at Black Hops HQ, it was now Govs' time to shine, and like a kid with a new Lego set, he got straight into piecing it all together. We'd chosen to remove a lot of the automated processes from our brewhouse, so there was a lot of extra piping that needed to be put in the right places. After a solid two days of hard piping, it was starting to take shape.

Unless you have a lot of experience with brewing equipment, it's best to leave this up to the professionals, and most brewing equipment suppliers offer installation as part of the package.

There are travel and accommodation costs involved, and so for us, Govs was keen to take it on himself.

Once he had it all set up, he noticed the sight glasses were missing. A quick phone call to Tiantai revealed that they had stored them in the hard-pipes, which were now all assembled!

It turns out they did label the pipes, but I guess Govs' Mandarin isn't so good. A few swear words and two hours later and the missing sight glasses were found.

Our first reactions were all very positive to the quality of the equipment. Everything was where it was supposed to be, and the quality of the workmanship was above expectations.

We then had to go through a long process of getting power to all of the pumps and controllers.

One issue we ran into was that all of the wiring diagrams were in Chinese, so we had to get them translated. Another issue was that it is not a legal requirement to have earth cables on electrical components in China, so we had to install them on everything. This is not a huge task but did cost us to have it done. We informed Tiantai that this is law in Australia, and they now do it as standard.

The next challenge was piping the glycol system together to make it all work. Govs hand-cut and welded every single PP-R pipe, elbow, valve, and tee-piece for the 40-metre-long glycol system, and then connected it up to the glycol tank and our two chilling units. This was a mammoth task and took the best part of two weeks to complete. We contacted our local cooling system specialist to fill and test the chillers and discovered there was some significant wiring changes that needed to be made. This, along with several hundred litres of glycol, cost us about $7,000. But, boy, did it work well afterwards!

We opted to play it safe and go for two chillers as a redundancy in case of breakdown and to lower the load, and this proved to be wise.

It didn't take us long before we were running water through the system, but it was a while before it was beer. The only piece of the puzzle remaining was heating.

As for after-sales support from Tiantai, it was very satisfactory. We haven't had to contact them many times but when we have, our questions have been answered usually within 24 to 48 hours. In one instance, we did need an urgent response when one of the parts used to weld the PP-R glycol pipes together was supplied in the incorrect size. Once we asked, a replacement part was shipped express to us that day from China. In another instance, we burned out the PP-R pipe socket welder using it for a whole day. The instructions said to only use it for 10 minutes at a time, but again, they were in Chinese. Tiantai quickly sent over a new one without charge.

Since placing our order, we have received emails from upcoming breweries all over the world looking for equipment suppliers, and it has been a great pleasure for us to share our journey.

We would recommend using Tiantai given all of the caveats we've already mentioned. If you do, please tell them Black Hops sent you. If you have any more questions about equipment, search for the Black Hops Ambassador group on Facebook. It's free to join, and we are regularly discussing equipment and brewery setup topics in there.

CHAPTER 12

APPROVALS

Getting equipment set up is one thing, getting all of the approvals is another. This is a minefield and it's going to be different in your location, so plan this part out well and get good advice. The biggest killer in these projects is time so start this process as early as you can.

Here is a quick list of everything we needed and what was involved.

Liquor licence

In our location, to sell alcohol, you need a producer wholesale licence. We got ours early on when we were contract brewing and had it assigned to Eddie's house. Getting the licence required filling in a stack of forms and about $1,500. It also required us to complete the Responsible Management of a Licenced Venue (RMLV) course.

It wasn't a huge job, but it did take a month or two to organize. When we wanted to move it to our new location, this was a bigger job. We hoped we could simply transfer it, but unfortunately, we had to put up a sign and go through an approval process.

We had a few prior issues with neighbours, so we were kind of expecting it to cause a few problems. In the end, no one objected, and a month later we had our licence.

Excise licence

To produce alcohol, you need an excise licence. In Australia, you get this by submitting a thick wad of forms to the ATO.

It is a massive component in the cost of brewing beer and requires you to keep very accurate records and submit your procedures to the ATO.

If you make home-brewed beer for non-commercial purposes using non-commercial equipment, you don't need an excise licence and don't need to pay excise duty.

The definition for beer can be found on the ATO website. Essentially, it's classified as a fermented beverage made from predominantly malted cereals that may also contain other sources of carbohydrates. It must contain hops or hop extract and be no less than four IBU and have more than 1.15% ABV.

You should be able to establish whether your product meets the definition of beer for excise purposes from your manufacturing specifications and processes and from standard industry information.

Excise duty rates in Australia are expressed per litre of alcohol for alcoholic beverages. The volume of alcohol is calculated by multiplying the actual volume of product by its alcoholic strength. For beer, the first 1.15% of alcohol content is free of excise duty.

They are indexed twice a year in line with the Consumer Price Index (CPI), generally on February 1 and August 1.

Unless you have periodic settlement permission, you must lodge an excise return and prepay excise duty before you deliver beer into the Australian domestic market. Once payment is received and approved, the ATO issue you a delivery authority allowing you to physically move the goods from the licenced premises and deliver them for domestic consumption.

Getting the licence wasn't a huge amount of work, but there were some things the ATO wanted to see like:

- Security - The ATO want to know that you secured your premises as best you can. We installed a back-to-base alarm system, security cameras, sensor lights, and additional locks on all roller doors.
- Packaging process - You need to show how you regulate your fill volumes on kegs.
- Testing and record keeping process - The ATO will want to see that you have adequate procedures in place to brew beer and are able to keep accurate records of production and testing for calculating ABV. There are a number of options for testing ABV. The easiest and most expensive is an Alcoholiser, but alternatively you can use ATO-approved hydrometers to calculate starting and finishing gravity.

Understanding all of this is critical if you want to run a brewery. The ATO website is a good source of information. If you are outside of Australia, chat with industry people and figure out where to go to learn about the equivalent for your region.

Food licence

In our area you don't need a dedicated licence to make beer, but because beer is considered food, you do need a food licence. This caused a few stressful moments because they treat the whole brewery like it's a kitchen and had some odd rules about what we needed to do. At one point, we were thinking we might have to put fly screens on our roller doors!

We didn't need the fly screens, but we did need to do a few things like:

- Filling every gap in sight (Eddie became a weapon on the silicon gun)
- Sealing any exposed timber
- Re-painting the floors
- Putting rubber sections above the garage door to close the gaps
- Siliconing the gaps in the cellar door tap wall, which took away a bit from the rustic look

One of the most sucky things was that we had to put a coat of clear sealant over the taproom doors. I messaged Matt, our designer, to see if he thought it would impact the logo he'd done. He said he didn't think it would, so Eddie and Govs started coating the wall. As soon as the brush went over the "Br" in "Brewery," the logo started running. Govs quickly tried to clean it up, but you could see the damage.

Matt came in and had a look, but we decided we'd do more harm than good if we tried to fix it. If you come into the brewery, you might notice the BR isn't perfect, but it's part of our story now.

RSA and RMLV

All three of us had to do the Responsible Service of Alcohol (RSA) course which was an online course filled with sometimes-cringeworthy questions about serving alcohol. $25 and 25 minutes later, we all knew not to sell shots to 12 year olds.

The RMLV course is a more involved course that proved to be a bit more useful. To operate a licenced premise, you need to have someone assigned as the bar manager, and this person must hold the RMLV certificate. In our case, this was Eddie, and he attended the two-day course.

Partnership agreement/shareholder agreement

When we first thought up the idea to start Black Hops, I drew up a simple partnership agreement between the three of us. This was fine in the early days, but not enough for a proper business with investors.

When we got investors, we paid a lawyer and accountant to set up a Pty Ltd company and draft a shareholder agreement to lodge with our local authority, ASIC (Australian Securities and Investments Commission).

Knowing accountants and lawyers helps. Spending money on this stuff isn't that much fun, but getting the right advice avoids trouble in the future.

Trademarks

Early on, we started looking into trademarks. It was a hot topic in the Australian scene because Monster Mash had recently had to re-name to Kaiju after a run-in with the Monster Energy drink company and Thunder Road and Stone & Wood were in a stoush over the beer "Pacific Ale."

We got some good advice from a trademark attorney and decided to trademark our main name and beer names in Australia with a view to possibly doing it in other regions after we were established.

Insurance

Insurance is also a must when you are running a brewery. We shopped around a little bit and decided pretty quickly that we wanted someone who had experience in the industry. We went with a company called Midland Insurance because they are listed as recommended by the Craft Beer Industry Association (CBIA) for breweries and some of our other brewery owner mates used them.

We are insured for regular events like burglary, fires, and floods, and also brewery-specific events like infected batches.

Council DA

Everything you need to do in order to open a brewery hinges on your Development Application (DA), so until the DA is approved, you aren't really progressing with anything else. For example, plumbing approval, trade waste approval, liquor licence, food licence, excise licence etc. Delays with the DA often mean delays with your entire project.

Of course, all councils are different, so make sure you have an expert on call who knows your local council backwards.

In our case, our local area has two main zones where you'd have any chance of getting approval to build a brewery. Industry One is "Heavy Industrial." If we were to open in an Industry One location, we could have probably done so without any DA. We had looked at a few sites in Industry One; however, they weren't in great locations, so most of the places we looked at were in Industry Two.

Industry Two zoning is "Light Industrial," and allows for industrial uses with the approval of the Council.

To get into the details, we technically applied for a Development Permit for a Material Change of Use (MCU) for Industry and Manufacturers Shop.

In essence, we were seeking to change from the existing uses (which included a warehouse and motor vehicle repairs) to an industry use (i.e., the Brewery) and a Manufacturer's Shop (i.e., the Cellar Door). This all came down to what was identified in the planning scheme and we knew that (1) we wouldn't be able to simply open in this location without approval, and (2) as long as we followed what Council wanted, we should be fine to open with some restrictions. At the end of the day, it's an industrial location and our business has much lower impact than other existing or potential industrial uses.

There were quite a few compromises and the process was slow. There were definitely moments where we wondered if we'd taken too much of a risk with this location.

The Cellar Door revolves around the Manufacturer's Shop defini-tion. To operate a conventional bar would technically fall under the Tavern definition. A Tavern would have required a more oner-ous impact-assessable application which would have been open to third-party objection and appeal. The Manufacturer's Shop definition limits the size of the area and limits products sold to those manufactured on site.

In layman's terms, as long as our tasting room was small, we were fine to sell beer made on-site. In the end, there were a few other restrictions as well, and some things we had to debate with Council.

The steps we undertook were:

1. Attend a pre-lodgement meeting with Council (albeit regarding the earlier site in Currumbin)
2. Lodge the application with Council
3. Respond to an information request from Council
4. Attend a meeting with the local Councillor and surrounding residents to address concerns
5. Meet with Council regarding some outstanding issues
6. Receive/review the approval

The initial Council meeting is optional but generally recommended to clarify any questions you have and get an indication of Council support before you spend a lot of money on plans/reports.

The meeting with neighbours was unusual for this type of application and was largely driven by the level of opposition from a few active local residents. The meeting went well; most people were assuming the impact would be a lot bigger than it was. After that first meeting, it has been smooth sailing with our neighbours so far.

Parking was a big issue. Cafes in the area had caused parking shortages and Council's Transport Department actually recommended the application be refused. Fortunately, it was overruled by the Planning Department.

The timeframe from lodgement to approval was five months, which is a bit more than we expected but we got there in the end without too many crazy restrictions. At one stage, the Council were going to allow us to have a bar but no bar stools. We told them that was fucking crazy, and, thankfully, they came around.

In the end, we had our draft DA signed off in January, which allowed us to proceed. It gave us a checklist for the next few months of works: plumbing, trade waste, licences, landscaping, conditions, etc.

Here is a short list of some of the requirements we had to cover:

- Plumbing - An approved hydraulic plumbing plan is required before you can have a plumber begin work. We worked with local engineer "Trouty" to come up with our plan. This includes mapping out everything from toilets, taps, and basins, as well as drainage and trade waste. This was a lengthy process as the plan then goes to Council and takes close to a month to pass through. Once you have the signed plans, you can begin plumbing.
- Trade waste - A trade waste licence and system, which took weeks of planning and was inspected multiple times.
- Landscaping for the front carpark - With an MCU, Council take the opportunity to ensure you make the street frontage better than it previously was. A plan needs to be submitted to Council by a licenced landscape architect and approved. They will want to know mulch depths, drainage, and species of trees.
- Lines for dedicated carparks - One of our biggest issues around the cellar door capacity and opening hours was our lack of on-site parking. We created six parks on our site and were required to have them marked out.

- Food licence - The food licence we talked about earlier was also part of the DA requirements.
- Audio - A sound test was required to make sure we weren't making too much noise. Again, this was done by a professional and was not an insignificant expense.
- Gas - We required a gas certificate for our steam generator and attached gas appliance.

For us, it was a lot of time delays and costs, but we expected some of that when we chose the location. Everything's a compromise, and we are very happy with where we ended up and what we ended up with. The Council wasn't unreasonable for the most part; there was just a lot of boxes to tick off.

CHAPTER 13

FUCKUPS

To go from drinking beer at the pub to opening our own brewery, we knew there were going to be mistakes along the way.

Some of them turned into fun stories for us to share afterwards and didn't impact us too much. Others hurt us badly and ultimately caused significant budget blowouts, timeframe extensions, and a lot of intense and stressful moments.

$115,000 over budget

We had aimed to build our brewery for a total cost of $300,000 AUD (not including working capital). In the end, it cost around $415,000. It's hard to pinpoint exactly where the additional charges were, but there were a few big ones:

1. We were about six months later than our ambitious goals. We were in our venue for 10 months and paying equipment rental and wages for six months. This ended up costing $50,000 or more in unexpected costs. In hindsight, our timeframe was too ambitious. We needed a much longer

rent-free period, and probably didn't all need to be working on it full-time for 10 months.

2. The boiler cost us a lot more than budgeted and also caused some of the above delays.
3. We had budgeted $27,000 for plumbing and trade waste. It ended up being over $70,000.
4. We budgeted $6,000 for electrical. It ended up being $11,000.
5. We budgeted $1,700 to set up the glycol. It ended up being $7,000.
6. The cellar door actually came in under budget because Martin pretty much built the whole thing for nothing.
7. We had a contingency of $30,000 (10%), but that disappeared very quickly. For a project this size, with no experience building anything like it, we needed a much higher contingency.

Also, keep in mind that we had a lot of free and "mates rates" work done on-site.

We thought we'd go over in some areas and under in others, but we really just went over in most areas. It was very hard to save money without making pretty significant compromises, and without the ability to brew and sell beer profitably, we couldn't make up the buffer.

The Pozible campaign helped, but even the injection of $18,000 wasn't enough to get us open.

It's hard to work out the exact costs because we were also contract brewing and selling beer at the time, but here is a rough guide of where it ended up:

Overall	Planned	Actual	Brewery setup	Planned	Actual
Brewing equipment	$140,000	$140,000	Plumbing	$15,000	$60,000
Delivery	$24,000	$27,000	Walls	$2,500	$2,500
Kegs	$3,542	$4,652	Electrical	$6,000	$11,000
Venue fitout	$19,000	$15,000	Tradewaste	$12,000	$11,500
Council	$20,000	$20,000	Carpentry	$3,000	$3,000
Total brewery setup	$51,200	$139,500	Security	$1,500	$1,500
Contingency	$43,000		Extra	$2,500	$2,500
Landscaping		$5,000	Paint	$4,000	$5,500
Delays		$50,000	Boiler setup	$3,000	$35,000
Call of Duty		$12,000	Glycol	$1,700	$7,000
Sound		$2,000			
Total	$300,742	$415,152			
Working capital	$30,000	$30,000			

In the end, we had to put more money in ourselves, and go back to our investors for another small round of funding. It wasn't satisfying to do, but we couldn't avoid it. To get what we have for $400,000 is really not that bad, and we think in the long term that the location will be worth the extra effort.

Oops, forgot the forklift

We were so excited when our equipment arrived at Christmas in 2015, but we also had a lot of work to do. We had to figure out how to get it all out using just a forklift and move it into the space for the brewery. And for each container, we only had one day before the truck took it away and replaced it with another one.

When the first one was due to arrive, we got the area ready and organised to have it dropped off right next to the second roller door so we could carry it straight in.

We filmed them dropping the container off the truck and posed for selfies in front of our new shiny equipment. Then we set about planning how we'd get the equipment out and into the brewery.

The first step was to lower the first tank down with our forklift. Govs went to get the forklift, but the problem was that the fork-lift was in Unit 1, and the new container was so long that it went straight past the roller door entrance to the unit. On top of that, the forklift was too high to drive between Units 1 and 2 where the equipment was to go. With a day to move all of our equipment out of the container, the forklift was stuck inside Unit 1. Luckily, Govs was able to open the roller door and push the forklift into the huge 40-foot container. After a few tries, he was able to move the con-tainer out of the way slightly to squeeze the forklift out the side. If you visit our brewery, you can still see the scrape marks on the bitu-men driveway. Sorry, Biebs, but crisis averted!

Next-Week-Pete and the bargain boiler from Bendigo

As we got our equipment into place and the plumbing sorted, our attention turned to our boiler. You probably know that in order to make beer you need hot water.

There are many options to do this when planning your brewhouse, such as electric, direct fire, and steam. We decided on steam because it's more controllable and efficient. Our boiler produces steam that is pumped throughout the jacketed HTL, mash, and kettle, heat-ing up whatever is inside it, such as water or wort.

When we planned our equipment, we were advised not to order the boiler from China and to source one locally instead. We looked around for a while and a cheap one came up at a carpet company in Bendigo. It was $3,000 and the right size to heat our system, but we'd have to pay to deliver it to the Gold Coast. Because we were still months out from getting the keys, we had to store it.

Once we got access, we moved the boiler from storage into the brewery, and it sat there for a while as we finalised the other parts of the process.

Prior to making the purchase, we had spoken to a person who had regularly serviced the boiler who said it was old but solid. But it was always a bit of an unknown. We didn't know for sure if it would work, and we didn't know how long it would take to set up or how much it would cost. We assumed that it would be pretty quick and easy and not cost us too much. We assumed wrong.

Our plumber did all he could to get it ready but we needed an expert steam and gas provider to get it up and running and certified. Our plumber told us he knew someone who was good, and he would come back in next week to check it out. Let's call him Pete—because that was his name.

Well, next week came around, and he was called off to another project. We had a few other things to do at this time, so we weren't too worried, and he said he'd come next week.

Next week came and when he came to check out the boiler he found that it was designed for the wrong type of gas, natural instead of LPG. He was going to have to re-jet it to work with the new gas, so he took the parts and said he'd bring them back next week.

Next week came, and the parts hadn't returned yet, so he said he'd come in next week.

That was the last we heard from him for a few months. We were busy chasing other things because there were other issues holding us up, but as we got closer to opening, we started chasing a bit harder.

It was a few months before Pete returned to make the final fixes to the boiler. When he rocked up, he found the electrics didn't work, so we had to get an electrician in to troubleshoot the electrics. This time it was Doorbell; Mushy wasn't available. Once that was done, they tried to turn the boiler on and found that the whole unit responsible for the gas jets was faulty.

We could either replace a few jets and hope that fixed it or replace the whole gas jet unit at a cost of $4,500. Either way, Pete said it would be done next week. The boiler was now one of the final things we needed before we could open. By this time, we'd re-named him "Next-Week-Pete" and we were seriously concerned that next week would come around and we'd still have no boiler.

Next week was the week of the GABS festival in Melbourne, and we were all desperate to tell everyone at GABS that we were open.

We considered buying a new one, hiring one, or giving Pete one more chance to fix our current one. The only chance of having it done before GABS was through Pete, so we decided to replace the whole gas jet unit, and Pete said he would bring it back in next week.

Next week came around, and the part was not sent back on time (apparently), so Pete once again told us he would come back, of course, next week.

We got drunk because by this time we were months delayed, had gone back for more investment money because we were so far over budget, and were embarrassed that we had not yet opened. Over a few (too many) beers, we decided to give him until the following Tuesday to get the part back to us, or we would pull the pin and get a new boiler.

At this time, we had probably spent $20,000 on the boiler in original purchase price, transport, storage, and parts and labour, and thousands more in delays for not opening. Our original $3,000 bargain had become the boiler from hell.

Next week came, and Pete wasn't contactable. We heard some information through a third party, but we couldn't talk to him directly. He had health issues as well and wasn't responding to calls or texts. We couldn't keep going this way, so we decided to get a new company out to look at the boiler.

Pete had been asked through the third party to provide us with the $5,000+ in parts that had been ordered and he refused.

We were then looking at re-ordering the parts and working with the new company when Pete called. He told us he could come and sort it out. You guessed it. Next fucking week.

By this time, we'd had enough and just wanted him out of our life. We told him if he didn't return the parts, he would wear the cost, and we would move forward with the next company.

We arranged another company, East Coast Steam, to come in and look at the boiler and they told us they could have it up and running within a week. As it turned out, they had to re-do a lot of Next-Week-Pete's work, but they were able to get it up and running by the following Thursday.

In the end, we spent a lot more than expected, and the stress almost killed us. If we could go back, we would buy a new one. It would probably cost a bit more, but that is something we don't want to experience ever again.

Packaging fail

The experience brewing a beer with the largest game on earth was something we'll never forget. There was, however, one big lesson in there.

As we got closer to planning the release of the beer, we started to delve into the requirements for the packaging. Activision looked after the design, but we paid for all of the six packs, cartons and bottle labels to be printed.

We had already negotiated the price before the packaging, and at this point, there was no going back. When we got the quote in from the packaging supplier, it was unprofitable for us to only do enough for one batch or 5,000 litres of beer. At this point, Activision had only committed to doing one brew, but we all thought it would be a huge success, and they had said they were keen to do more than one.

Packaging wise, it was only a small amount more to do enough for two batches and doing so would mean we would break even on the deal. If we did one lot, we would lose thousands of dollars on this batch and would have to re-negotiate any more batches if we didn't want to lose money on those. We took the chance and ordered enough packaging for two batches, but soon after launching, it became clear that they wouldn't be doing any more than the one batch.

In the end, we lost over $10,000 on the deal which stung at the time. In hindsight, the attention we got from that was probably worth a lot more than $10,000, but that's a lot of money to lose while trying to build a brewery on a crazy-tight budget.

Relying on friends

We had some absolute legends help us out on the brewery. Where we could, we called on friends for anything from painting to plumbing, electrical, engineering, design, and every trade you can imagine.

Working with friends is great, and we are so grateful for the help we got. We still wanted to mention that sometimes it's not easy working with friends, and ideally on a project like this, you have the right amount of money to be able to pay for the experts you need. Beer is the ultimate currency, but working with friends can get complicated.

For us, if we do this again, we'd make sure we had enough money to pay the people we need to do the work then just invite our friends around to enjoy it.

That's the best-case scenario, but when do you ever have more money than you need for a project?

CHAPTER 14

OPENING DAY

It was 11:00 a.m. Friday June 17, 2016. Govs ran up to Eddie and said, "The boiler is working; we're brewing tomorrow! Twelve months of planning, spending, painting, lots of painting, stress, beers, and fun had come down to us deciding to brew, launch, and open with zero notice.

This isn't really how we had imagined it would go down. We assumed we'd have a week or two to play with some boiling water in the comfort of knowing we had come in under budget and with time to spare. This was far from the case. In fact, the three of us weren't even all there.

In the last 12 months, I hadn't organised a single trip away for more than a few days, opting to stay close to HQ as we got it up and running.

My trip to the U.S. was locked in months in advance, and I was certain we'd be open by the time it came around. Unfortunately, we weren't, and on the Friday the boiler was commissioned, I was in a meeting in San Francisco.

We had all agreed that we'd open the second we could brew, so the stage was set for a rushed first brew and tasting room opening the next day.

With opening plans in place, the conversation quickly turned to what we would brew. As part of the Pozible campaign, we promised Beach House would be the first beer brewed, but with zero notice and yeast to prepare, we had two options: hold off brewing until the following week or brew something else.

Eggnog Stout was our first beer as Black Hops, we had everything we needed to brew it, so the boys decided to brew that.

They set about preparing the equipment for the next day including heating up the HTL, moving the hot liquor to the kettle, and bringing it to the boil. They cleaned the brewhouse vessels, prepped and cleaned the fermenter, and then filled the HLT again and brought it to temperature in readiness for the morning brew.

We posted a message on social media about opening the next day, and the post got a lot of attention. A few outlets released stories about our opening, and when Eddie and Govs finished up that night at about 9:00 p.m., there was a buzz about the launch the following day.

Eddie and Govs didn't sleep much that night. Eddie worried about mopping the floors, RSAs being printed, and having the cellar door looking nice. Govs worried about all of the shit that could go wrong with a rushed brew. I was somewhere in the Mission in San Francisco smashing Pliny on tap to celebrate. I slept fine.

They met at 6:00 a.m. Saturday to begin milling. It was going well, all of the pale malt milled no worries—then the mill stopped. Shit! The motor was too hot to touch and the plastic fan began to melt and was literally dripping off. The boys put it in the cold room to try to cool it down and try again, but that didn't help. It just wouldn't turn on; it was cooked.

They still had the black malt to mill, about 25 kg worth. They ended up taking off the belts and securing a set of multi grips to it to hand-mill the remaining black malt.

With all grain milled, it was time to mash. The brew went to plan, although it was a long brew day. Govs continued brewing as Eddie manned the cellar door for guests arriving well before the scheduled 12:00 p.m. opening time.

At 12:00 p.m., Eddie began pouring beers, and our tiny tasting room filled up with 30 to 40 people. For our opening day, from 12:00 until 4:00, it was packed the whole time with a good mix of beer industry people, locals, and friends.

It was an epic day with a great vibe. The boys met a lot of locals and made some new friends. It was everything we had hoped for; we'd finally opened our brewery.

Keep following the journey

Opening our brewery was just the beginning for us. Now the real works starts, and we're excited to continue sharing it with you.

Our brewery build hasn't been smooth sailing, but we've kept our promise of sharing every step along the way. We will continue to be the least covert operation in brewing, and we'll

Made in the USA
San Bernardino, CA
01 June 2018